Sea Fishing Ireland
Handbook
2009

Brian Kinsella

BK Publications

For Gillian

Published by BK Publications, Boleys Cross,
Kilmore, Co Wexford, Ireland

Published in 2008
© BK Publications
www.bkpublications.ie

© Ordnance Survey Ireland/Government of Ireland
Copyright Permit No. MP 006108
© Crown Copyright and/or database rights. Reproduced by permission of the Controller of Her Majesty's Stationery Office and the UK Hydrographic Office (www.ukho.gov.uk)
© www.solunar.com
© Central Fisheries Board

Contributing authors and photographers:
Cormac Walsh
Kevin Hanrahan
Kevin Braine
Roger O Bogaigh
Don Browse
Steven Turner
Conor Mountaine

Contributing Artist:
Rod Sutterby

Printed and bound in Thailand by:
Kyodo Nation Printing Services Co., Ltd

CONTENTS

ACKNOWLEDGEMENTS

I couldn't possibly list all of the names of those who contributed to this book, the list would be a book on its own! All I can do is thank everybody for their kind help, particularly the anglers who provided local information on their marks around Ireland. These people have fished the areas for years and are far more knowledgeable on their marks than I ever could be.

I would like to thank the Central Fisheries Board for allowing me permission to use material from their publications, Nizan in Mactackle.com for his help and advice, and Angela in Murphy's Tackle, for the supply and help with fishing tackle throughout the years.

I would also like to thank my good friend Cormac Walsh for his help and contributions to the book and my brother Bobby and friend Paul for their help and distractions (without which I probably would have lost my sanity). Thanks also to my other fisherman friends, Jamie, Neil, Bruno and Richard who, through their existence, always ensure I have someone to go fishing with.

I must also mention my father Marty, my uncle John, Tony and Marty McBride, and Michael Busher, for had they not shared their wisdom with me throughout the years, this book would never have been written.

I would like to thank the rest of my family, my mother and two sisters and my future in-laws for all their support and loose change when times were tough!

Finally and most importantly I have to thank my beautiful Fiancée Gillian for all her support and patience. The sacrifices she has made over the past year to allow me time to write this book can never be repaid.

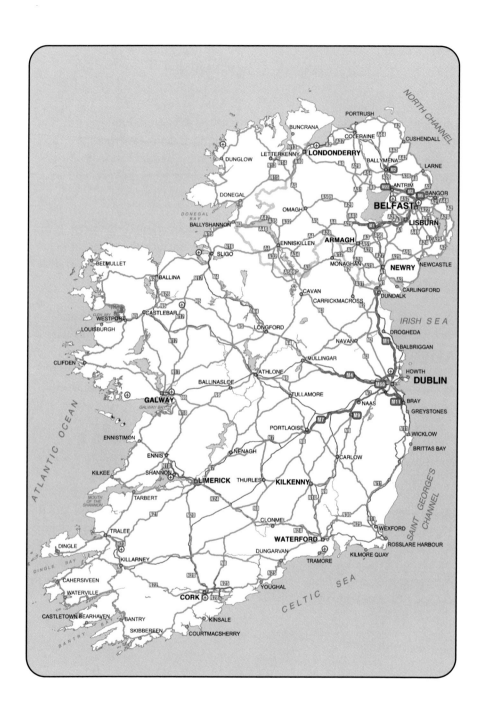

INTRODUCTION

The world is a very different place. Cities are growing. Buildings steal the horizon and concrete paves our old grass walkways. With so many people, it's hard to find space to breath. People don't know their neighbours, and text and email have replaced the age old art of conversation.

But there is still a place where the sun shines bright, lighting up anyone's darkest day. Where a fresh breeze blows all the troubles from your mind, and a cleansing air that can lift even the greatest weight from your shoulders. As long as our fish, seas and coastline are protected, we will always have a place of solitude or a chance to swap fishing yarns with a companion, an escape to nature and a chance of catching the fish of a lifetime.
Can you think of a better place?

The Sea Fishing Ireland Handbook 2009 has been written to assist all anglers, young and old, in their development of fishing techniques and knowledge of the sport. I hope it will serve as a point of reference for any information that anglers need throughout the 2009 year and also promote Ireland's extensive range of fish and marks.

Ireland boasts such a diverse range of marine species, possibly the greatest in Europe, and coupled with an endless choice of fishing locations, provides every angler in Ireland with fishing possibilities second to none.

I hope all of you anglers, locals and visitors, will find my book helpful in your fishing expeditions and assist you in your quest for the big one.

Brian Kinsella
September 2008

SPINNING

Spinning is a form of fishing where an artificial lure is attached to the line on your rod and reel, and continually cast out and retrieved. This type of fishing is suitable for predatory fish and is most commonly used when fishing for Bass, Sea Trout, Pollock and Salmon. There are a number of reasons why spinning is my favourite form of fishing. Don't get me wrong, I love shore angling with bait, boat angling and fly fishing, but if I were to fish seven days a week, at least 5 of them would be spinning. It is the ease of just getting up, grabbing my rod, reel, waders and a box of spinners and driving to a decent spot that 'lures' me to spinning, pardon the pun! I know this can be said of fly fishing also, however, the ability to spin is less reliant on the weather than fly fishing is. Travelling light is great, as you can explore a decent stretch of coast-line while spinning, that you probably wouldn't otherwise see if you were bait fishing. To explore a coastline as extensively would entail walking the shores at low and high tide looking for marks, and let's be honest, if I was doing this, I would sooner have a rod in my hand than just twiddling my thumbs!

As you usually use fairly light tackle when spinning, catching a fish is always a great adrenaline rush, even a small fish will bend the rod over. Like fly fishing, you are almost stalking the fish, ensuring you are using the right lure, casting to where the fish are holding, and retrieving the lure at the right speed, in the right way.

What rod do I use?

So often I see people on the beach spinning an 18-25 gram lure with a big beach casting outfit, suitable for an 8 oz weight. It makes no difference to the fish what gear you use, if they like the look of the spinner they will go for it.

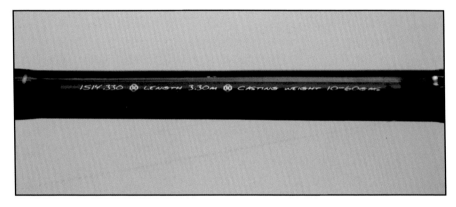

However, using big heavy gear like this takes a lot of enjoyment out of spinning. With the right gear, you would hardly feel the weight of the rod and reel, and you could fish for hours with ease. Also, as the casting weights of beach casting rods are suitable for heavy weights, it is likely you are not going to cast your lure past 30 yards. A lot of the time, fish are within this short distance, but sometimes you will need to go further.

When choosing a rod to spin with, first check the specifications. These are usually written above the butt. In the case of most sea spinning, a rod designed for 18-60 gram lures is perfect; however, there are lighter rods more suited to lighter lures and heavier rods for heavier lures. The next thing to check is the length of the rod. Spinning rods come in various lengths but most commonly found between 8 and 10 feet. I usually use a 10 foot rod myself as the added length provides a greater cast when spinning out to far off rocks from the shore; however, shorter rods are more suitable to spinning off a boat or on the bank of a river where casting space might be restricted. Put simply, only use a longer rod if you feel you will need the added distance, otherwise use a shorter rod as it is a little easier to handle.

And a reel?

You will be looking for a very light reel to use for spinning. There are mainly two types available; a multiplier type reel and the more common fixed spool reel. The multiplier type reel is newer, usually providing greater casting distance due to the lack of friction. As the spool is horizontal, it spins when casting allowing the line to come off without a lot of friction, but it is difficult to control the cast, as very often, the spool will turn too quickly causing the line to unravel which forms a 'birds nest' on the reel. This can take a long time to clear from the reel, and with very light line or braid, sometimes becomes

Multiplier type spinning reel   *Fixed spool spinning reel*

impossible to clear. The fixed spool I find is more suited to spinning as it is effortless to maintain while fishing, and when used with good line, will rarely pose any problem.

Reels are very complex nowadays and I find that any spinning reels I have bought for €6 to €10 can be very hit and miss. They might seem fine in the shop, but after a day's spinning with a dodgy one, you will wish you forked out a little more for a decent reel. The specifications for reels are usually written on the side of the reel, giving you an idea how much of a certain size line it will hold e.g. LINE CAP. (lbs – yds) 8-240   10-200   12-160. This would mean that the reel will hold 240 yards of 8lb line etc. This, along with the size of the reel itself, is how you would know a spinning reel from larger bait fishing reels that would have line capacity specifications for much heavier line. I have personally always used Shimano reels for spinning. They are perfectly balanced and the line lay is excellent. If you decide to use braid, ensure your reel has good line lay i.e., when you reel the line in, it is all laid onto the spool evenly.

What line will I load it with?

When buying line for your reel, always try to buy as light as possible. The lower the breaking strain of the line, the lower the diameter, which in turn allows for greater casting distance as there is less wind resistance. There are lots of different lines out there that usually fall under two categories; mono and braid. Mono is the standard line that has been used for years. It is easy to handle and fairly cheap. Braid is a newer type of line that consists of

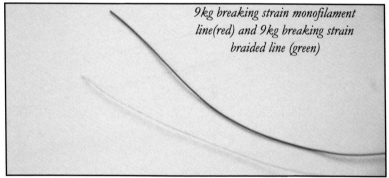

9kg breaking strain monofilament line(red) and 9kg breaking strain braided line (green)

braided fibres. It is much stronger than mono line, and has a much smaller diameter, and, in turn leads to longer casts. It doesn't have any stretch which allows the angler to feel almost everything the lure touches as it is retrieved. However, as braided line is opaque, which means it can be seen in the water, a lot of angers tend to attach clear mono leader to the end of the line to ensure the fish do not see anything attached to the lure. I used to load my reel with 8lb mono line when spinning however in more recent years I have changed to braid. The choice really depends on the angler.

Ok, I have it all, now what's the best lure?

This really is the fun part! I can't tell you what the best lures are as there are literally thousands of lures to choose from and it will be the ones that you catch the fish on, that you will stick with forever. Well that's how it is with mine anyway. Lures fall into 2 main categories:

Spinners/Spoons are usually metallic and when retrieved, move like a fish and flash light off them to attract predators. These generally don't fish too deep, however you can adjust the depth at which they are fished my speeding up or slowing down your retrieve. Some have a spinning mechanism around the main body to add extra flash in the retrieve.

The spinners/spoons below and on the following page are some of the more popular lures. All of them work equally well in their own way and I have had a lot of success with all of them with several different species of fish caught on most.

Kilty Catcher	**Toby**
Metallic, flashes light and imitates sandeel or sprat. Standard retrieve. Fishing depth varies with retrieve speed.	*Wobblier than the Kilty, imitating more so an injured fish. Standard retrieve. Fishes shallow but depth can vary.*

Skarpsilda

Sprat-like fishing action, can be improved by jerking the rod. Excellent for Sea Trout. Fishing depth varies also.

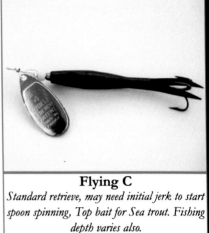

Flying C

Standard retrieve, may need initial jerk to start spoon spinning, Top bait for Sea trout. Fishing depth varies also.

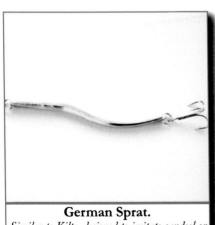

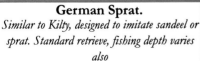

German Sprat.

Similar to Kilty, designed to imitate sandeel or sprat. Standard retrieve, fishing depth varies also

Jensen Pirken

Darting sprat like fishing action, needs assistance by jerking the rod. Great for Sea Trout. Fishing depth varies also.

Plugs are a hard bodied lure that are becoming more and more popular. They can be hollow and solid, come in numerous sizes, shapes and colours, some looking so flashy, you would never think they would tempt a fish. However, they have shown to be probably the most productive type of lure for fishing.

Surface plugs: these float on top of the water and are designed to resemble an injured fish. It is a spectacular sight to see a bass breaking the water to attack these lures. As with all spin and lure fishing, the retrieve is very important with surface plugs as you need to ensure that what you are doing does in fact resemble an injured fish.

Shallow divers, medium divers and deep divers: Each of these can be used for different fish in different situations. The depth at which the plugs fish depends on the angle of the vane at the head of the body. Quite often, it will tell you on the packaging how deep the lure will fish, so you can make your decision based on this. The shallow divers are suitable for fishing over shallow ground, where fish may be feeding and where you need to stay near the surface to avoid losing your lure in rocks. Deep diving plugs are suitable for deep water and can fish very varying depths. They are usually retrieved by just reeling in, as the body of the lure is designed to imitate a fish or eel. The following are examples of some of the more popular types of plugs

Shallow Diving 2ft-4ft	Surface Walker 0ft
	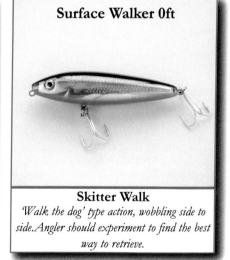
Tormentor	**Skitter Walk**
Shallow diving with holographic and rattle features Great swimming action when reeled at standard rate.	*'Walk the dog' type action, wobbling side to side. Angler should experiment to find the best way to retrieve.*

Subsurface Walker 0ft-2ft	Suspended/deep diving 6ft-15ft
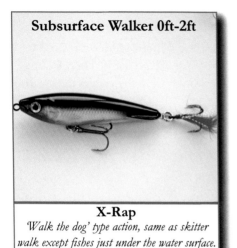	
X-Rap *'Walk the dog' type action, same as skitter walk except fishes just under the water surface.*	**Glass Shad Rap** *Glass technology picks up more light than other lures. Standard retrieve, but can remain suspended while twitching.*
Medium Diving 4ft-12ft	**Surface Popper 0ft**
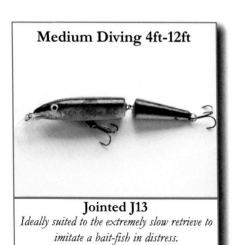	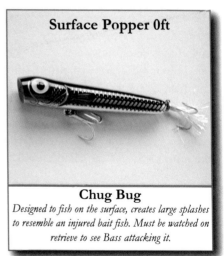
Jointed J13 *Ideally suited to the extremely slow retrieve to imitate a bait-fish in distress.*	**Chug Bug** *Designed to fish on the surface, creates large splashes to resemble an injured bait fish. Must be watched on retrieve to see Bass attacking it.*

As with all baits and lures, you will decide which you like best and if you are like me, you will probably end up with a box full of lures that you never use!

Finally a few tips

A lot of the time you will encounter weed when spinning. Once the weed is caught on your lure, it is extremely unlikely a fish will go for it. There's not a lot you can do to combat it, my suggestion would be, if the area is thick with weed, go somewhere else.

However, if the weed is not too thick, you can reduce the chance of it getting caught on your lure as shown to me by Arthur Daly by tying a size 12 (29lb) barrel swivel 2 to 3 feet up from your lure. You will find the weed catches in your main line a lot of the time, and runs down onto the lure. A swivel will sometimes catch this weed 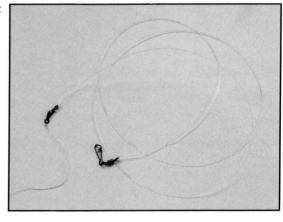 and hold it away from your lure. I find this is also useful when using braid on my main line. I tie my braided main line to the swivel, and then attach 2-3 feet of clear mono line to the other end of the swivel. As the clear mono cannot be seen by fish in the water, the lure looks more realistic seeming to be swimming by itself. I then attach a size 14 (20 lb) eye and snap swivel to the end of the mono line so I can change lures easily and quickly.

Also, get yourself a good pair of neoprene chest waders. These can be expensive, the lowest price probably being €80 - €90, but they will be worth it. You can explore more of the coastline in a pair of chest waders, you don't have to worry about getting wet, and most of all, they will keep you snug and warm, even in the cold of winter.

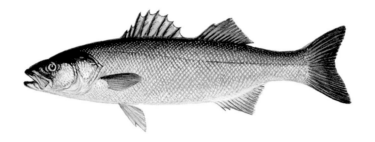

Bass Angling regulations

There are a number of regulations in place in relation to Bass fishing in Ireland. The minimum overall size limit of bass that can be kept is **40cm**, measured from tip of snout to the end of the tail. Commercial fishing for bass is prohibited, the taking of bass using nets is prohibited, and Irish fishing boats must not have bass on board or engage in transhipment of bass.

Bass Fishing Conservation Bye-law (Renewed annually)
The effect of this Bye-law is to impose a bag limit on anglers of two bass in any one period of 24 hours and to provide for a ban on angling for bass during the spawning season (15th May to the 15th June).

Bass (Restriction on Sale) Order, (Renewed annually)
The effect of this Order is to prohibit the sale or offer for sale of bass (other than bass which has been imported into the State) from 1st day of July to 30th day of June.

Note: Penalties for breach of the above laws include confiscation of tackle and heavy fines.

Suspected illegal Poaching:
Contact: Irish Bass Protection and Awareness Group
Website:www.irishbass.org
Text: 087-6406352
Email: report@irishbass.org

Rod Sutterby

Salmon

WILD SALMON AND SEA TROUT ANGLING REGULATIONS 2008

To fish for Salmon or Sea Trout in Ireland, you must first obtain a license. There are several restrictions in place in relation to Salmon and Sea Trout angling and certain rivers are restricted. Anglers can obtain their licence from Regional Fisheries Board headquarters, any rod licence distributor (usually your local tackle shop) or online at www.salmonlicences.ie. The prices of these licenses are reviewed annually.

Rod Sutterby

Sea Trout

The following information should be used as a guide to anglers in relation to restrictions on Salmon and Sea Trout Angling. However, the information is subject to change. All up to date regulations can be obtained from your local Regional Fisheries Board.

BAG LIMITS

There is an angling bag limit of 10 salmon (any size) or sea trout (over 40 cm) on rivers where you may catch and retain salmon (Table 1). The bag limits are subject to any quota allocated to a river and its tributaries.
Subject to the maximum annual bag limit of ten fish an angler may take:

•   Daily bag limit: One salmon (any size) or sea trout (over 40cm) per day for the period beginning January 1st to May 11th (three fish in total may be retained for this period).
•   Daily Bag Limit: Three salmon (any size) or sea trout (over 40cm) per day from May 12th to August 31st.
•   Daily Bag Limit: One salmon (any size) or sea trout (over 40cm) per day from 1st September to the close of the season.
•   Please note that no sea trout of any size caught in the Western Region or the Clew Bay area of the North Western Region can be retained.
After the daily bag limit has been taken, anglers are permitted to fish catch and release, using single barbless hooks and there is a ban on the use of worms.

On rivers where catch and release is permitted (Table 2):
•   there is a ban on the use of worms
•   anglers must use single barbless hooks
•   the fish must be handled carefully and should not be removed from the water prior to release.

On all other rivers (Table 3) angling for salmon (any size) and sea trout (over 40cm) is prohibited. On the Liffey, angling for all salmon (any size) and all sea trout (any size) is prohibited On the Slaney angling is restricted to catch & release for all salmon and all sea trout. The Newport River (Lough Beltra) & Garavogue River (Lough Gill and River Bonnet) provides for catch & release up to 11th May in order to protect spring fish with both rivers open for angling from 12th May.

Licence Pack

On payment of the rod licence fee, the angler will be given:
- The relevant rod licence.
- A logbook.
- Up to 10 gill tags where an (annual) ordinary, juvenile, or district licence shall be issued.
- 3 gill tags where a twenty one day ordinary licence shall be issued up until 11th May and additional allocations after this date up to a maximum of 10 gill tags in total provided they demonstrate that they have completed their logbook appropriately.
- 1 gill tag where a one day ordinary licence shall be issued up until 11th May, 3 gill tags from 12th May to 31st August and 1 gill tag from 1st Sept to the close of the season.
- A business reply envelope will be provided for return of the logbook and unused tags to the relevant Regional Fisheries Board.
- A plastic wallet for the logbook.

THE TAG

The tag to be used by anglers is a blue or brown plastic self-locking device. Each tag is embossed with a code identifying the region (or river and district) in which the tag was issued, the year in which the tag can be used and a tag number.

Fishermen should carefully note the following concerning the use of these tags:
- Each rod licence holder will be issued tags for his/her use only. Tags are not transferable between licence holders.
- These tags shall not be re-used.
- One tag shall be attached to each salmon (any size) and sea trout (over 40 cm) caught and retained.

- Tags must be attached immediately on landing the fish.
- Tags shall be attached through the gill opening and mouth and securely locked around the gill cover.
- Additional tags shall be issued on presentation of logbook information showing that the licence holder has used the gill tags issued to him or her, subject to bag limits.
- Lost and accidentally destroyed tags may be replaced upon presentation of a signed declaration completed by the angler and signed by an Authorised Officer of a Regional Fisheries Board.
- Gill Tags shall only be removed from the fish at the time of processing in accordance with the Tagging Scheme Regulations. For the purposes of this scheme, processing includes: smoking, marinating or cooking the fish, gutting and freezing the fish or cutting any steaks, cutlets or portions of the fish.

THE LOGBOOK

On receipt of tags, the angler will also receive a logbook. Details of the gill tags issued to an angler will be entered into the angler's logbook by the issuing agent.

Each fisherman shall:

- Have the logbook in his/her possession while fishing for salmon or sea trout.
- Record all details of their catch in their logbook immediately after tagging the fish.
- Make a catch record even if the fish is released.
- Record details of any lost or damaged tags.
- Declare lost or damaged logbooks to the relevant Regional Fisheries Board.

RETURNING LOGBOOKS AND UNUSED TAGS

In accordance with the Wild Salmon and Sea Trout Tagging Regulations anglers are required by law to return their completed logbook (even if there is no catch recorded) and all unused tags to the issuing Regional Fisheries Board by the 19th October of the relevant year. A business reply envelope is provided for this purpose. Anglers are required to obtain proof of postage and to retain such proof for 12 months.

Anglers are prohibited from selling salmon (any size) or sea trout (any size) caught by rod and line.

These guidelines have been prepared for information purposes only and do not purport to be a legal interpretation.

Table 1: Open Fisheries

Fishery district (1)	River (2)	Open date	Close Date	Notes
Lismore	Blackwater	01-Feb	30-Sep	
Cork	Owennacurra	01-Feb	30-Sep	Sea Trout Closing 12Oct
	Lower Lee	01-Feb	30-Sep	Sea Trout Closing 12Oct
	Bandon	15-Feb	30-Sep	
	Ilen	01-Feb	30-Sep	Sea Trout Closing 12Oct
	Mealagh	17-Mar	30-Sep	Sea Trout Closing 12Oct
	Coomhola	17-Mar	30-Sep	Sea Trout Closing 12Oct
Kerry	Roughty	15-Mar	30-Sep	Sea Trout Closing 12Oct
	Blackwater	15-Mar	30-Sep	
	Sneem	15-Mar	30-Sep	Sea Trout Closing 12Oct
	Waterville	17-Jan	30-Sep	
	Caragh	17-Jan	30-Sep	Sea Trout Closing 12Oct
	Laune	17-Jan	30-Sep	Sea Trout Closing 12Oct
	Owenmore R.	01-Apr	30-Sep	
	Sheen	15-Mar	30-Sep	Sea Trout Closing 12Oct

Limerick	Feale	01-Mar	30-Sep	
	Mulkear	01-Mar	30-Sep	
Galway *All sea trout must be released in Galway District*	Corrib	01-Feb	30-Sep	Sea Trout 1 Jun - 30 Sep
Connemara *All sea trout must be released in Connemara District*	Cashla	01-Feb	30-Sep	Sea Trout 1 Jun - 30 Sep
	Screebe	01-Feb	30-Sep	Sea Trout 1 Jun - 12 Sep
	Ballynahinch	01-Feb	30-Sep	Sea Trout 1 Jun - 30 Sep
Ballinakill *All sea trout must be released in Ballinakill District*	Erriff	01-Feb	30-Sep	Sea Trout 1 Jun - 12 Oct
	Bundorragha	01-Feb	30-Sep	Sea Trout 1 Jun - 30 Sep
	Owenglin (Clifden)	01-Feb	30-Sep	Sea Trout 1 Jun - 30 Sep
	Dawros	01-Feb	30-Sep	Sea Trout 1 Jun - 30 Sep
Bangor	Burrishoole	10-Jun	30-Sep	
	Owenduff	01-Feb	30-Sep	Sea Trout 1 Feb - 12 Oct
	Owenmore R.	01-Feb	30-Sep	
	<u>Newport R. (Lough Beltra)</u>*	20-Mar	30-Sep	Catch and release for salmon and sea trout to 11 May
Ballina	Moy	01-Feb	30-Sep	Cathedral Beat & down-stream opens 17 Apr
	Easkey	01-Feb	30-Sep	

Angling regulations

Sligo	Ballysadare	01-Mar	30-Sep	
	Drumcliff	01-Feb	30-Sep	Sea Trout 1 Feb - 12 Oct
	Garvogue (Lough Gill & River Bonnet)*	01-Feb	30-Sep	Catch and release for salmon and sea trout to 11 May
Ballyshannon	Duff	01-Feb	30-Sep	
	Drowes	01-Jan	30-Sep	
	Eany	01-Apr	30-Sep	Sea Trout 1 Mar - 9 Oct
	Glen	01-Mar	30-Sep	
Letterkenny	Owenea	01-Apr	30-Sep	
	Gweebarra	01-Apr	30-Sep	
	Crana	01-Mar	30-Sep	Sea Trout 1 Mar-12Oct
Dundalk	Fane	01-Apr	12-Oct	Sea Trout 1 Apr -30 Sep

*Newport and Garavogue Rivers:

Angling is restricted to catch and release in respect of Salmon and Sea Trout (over 40 cm) in the Newport River (Lough Beltra) and Garavogue River (Lough Gill and River Bonnet) during the period 1 January to 11 May in order to protect spring fish.

On rivers where catch and release is permitted (Table 2):
• 	There is a ban on the use of worms,
• 	Anglers must use single, barbless hooks,
• 	The fish must be handled carefully and should not be removed from the water prior to release.

	Table 2: Fisheries open to Catch and Release only			
Fishery District (1)	*River (2)*	*Open Date*	*Close Date*	*Notes*
Waterford District	*Nore*	*17-Mar*	*30-Sep*	
	Suir	*17-Mar*	*30-Sep*	
	Colligan	*17-Mar*	*30-Sep*	
Cork District	*Argideen*	*15-Feb*	*30-Sep*	*Sea Trout Closing 12 Oct*
	Owvane	*17-Mar*	*30-Sep*	*Sea Trout Closing 12 Oct*
	Adrigole	*17-Mar*	*30-Sep*	*Sea Trout Closing 12 Oct*
	Glengarriff	*17-Mar*	*30-Sep*	*Sea Trout Closing 12 Oct*
Kerry District	*Croanshagh*	*15-Feb*	*30-Sep*	*Sea Trout Closing 12 Oct*
	Inney	*17-Mar*	*30-Sep*	*Sea Trout Closing 12 Oct*
	Carhan	*01-Apr*	*30-Sep*	
	Ferta	*01-Apr*	*30-Sep*	
	Behy	*17-Jan*	*30-Sep*	*Sea Trout Closing 12 Oct*
	Maine	*17-Jan*	*30-Sep*	*Sea Trout Closing 12 Oct*
Connemara District *All sea trout must be released in Connemara District*	*L. Na Furnace*	*01-Feb*	*30-Sep*	*Sea Trout 1 Jun - 30 Sep*
Ballinakill District *All sea trout must be released in Ballinakill Distric*	*Carrownisky*	*01-Apr*	*30-Sep*	*Sea Trout 1 Jun - 30 Sep*
	Bunowen	*01-Apr*	*30-Sep*	*Sea Trout 1 Jun - 30 Sep*
	Owenwee	*01-Feb*	*30-Sep*	*Sea Trout 1 Jun - 30 Sep*
	Culfin	*01-Feb*	*30-Sep*	*Sea Trout 1 Jun - 30 Sep*

Angling regulations

Wexford	Slaney	10-Mar	31-Aug	Catch and release for salmon and all sea trout
Drogheda District	Boyne	01-Mar	30-Sep	
Dundalk District	Castletown	01-Mar	12-Oct	

The River Slaney:

River Slaney (Catch & Release) restricts angling to catch and release for salmon and all sea trout in the River Slaney.

On all other rivers **(Table 3)** angling for salmon (any size) and sea trout (over 40cm) is prohibited. Angling for salmon and all sea trout is prohibited in the River Liffey.

Table 3: Closed Fisheries

Fishery District (1)	River (2)
No. 1 or Dublin District	Dargle, Vartry, Liffey
No. 2 or Wexford District	Avoca, Owenavorragh
No. 3 or Waterford District	Black Water, Barrow, Corrock, Owenduff, Pollmounty, Linguan, Clodiagh, Mahon ,Tay
No. 4 or Lismore District	Bride, Lickey, Finisk, Glenshelane, Tourig, Womanagh
No. 5 or Cork District	Upper Le
No. 7 or Kerry District	Owenshagh, Finnihy, Owenascaul, Feohanagh, Cloonee, Owenreagh, Emlaghmore, Cottoners, Emlagh, Milltown, Lee (Kerry), Kealincha, Lough Fadda
No. 8 or Limerick District	Brick, Galey, Deel, Owenagarney, Skivileen, Aughyvackeen, Doonbeg, Annageeragh, Inagh, Fergus, Maigue, Shannon (excluding Mulkear)
No. 9(1) or Galway District	Clarinbridge, Knock, Aille, Owenboliska, Spiddal, Kilcolgan
No. 10(2) or Bangor District	Owengarve, Muingnabo

Brown gill tags

A system of brown gill tags is in place on certain rivers where it is considered necessary in the interests of conserving salmon stocks to closely monitor the angling quotas to ensure that river based quotas are not exceeded.

Anglers should use a brown gill tag in addition to their blue gill tag on the rivers listed opposite. Please contact the relevant Regional Fishery Board to request information on how to obtain additional brown gill tags.

Please note that the daily and annual bag limits still apply. List of Districts and Rivers to which these Regulations apply from 1 January to 11 May

Fishery District	Rivers	Tag Code
Cork - Contact SWRFB	Bandon	B1
Lismore- Contact SRFB	Blackwater (Munster)	C1

List of Districts and Rivers to which these Regulations apply from 1 January to 30 September

Fishery District	Rivers	Tag Code
Cork - Contact SWRFB	Lower Lee	K2
	Ilen	P2
Kerry - Contact SWRFB	Sneem	F2
	Sheen	T2
	Roughty	G2
	Owenmore	S2
Ballinakill - Contact WRFB	Erriff	N2
	Bundorragha	W2
Sligo - Contact NWRFB	Ballysadare	E2

Information is correct at the time of printing, Sep 08, however if in any doubt, please visit your local Regional Fisheries Board or www.salmonlicences.ie for up-to-date information.

CONSERVATION OF EEL FISHING
(Annual Close Season)

This Bye-law prohibits the taking or fishing for brown eel under 30cm in length. The Bye-law also provides for a close season for brown eel, from 1 September to 31 May of the following year. The Bye-law also provides for a close season for silver eel from 1 January to 30 September in any year.

Simple Knots and Rigs

Everyone knows, if you need a good knot, ask a fisherman!!

The following 3 knots are probably the most common knots for each of their purposes. Although there are variations of each knot, and many others that do the same job, these knots are probably the simplest and most reliable for their funtion.

Improved Clinch Knot

Also known as the Tucked half blood knot, this is one of the most commonly used knots by fishermen. It can be tied with either mono or braid and is mostly used for tying hooks, swivels and weight clips.

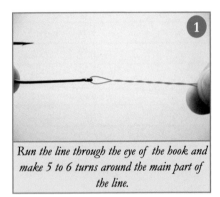

Run the line through the eye of the hook and make 5 to 6 turns around the main part of the line.

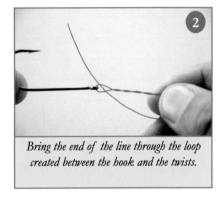

Bring the end of the line through the loop created between the hook and the twists.

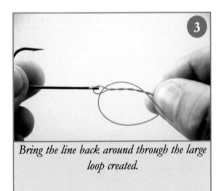

Bring the line back around through the large loop created.

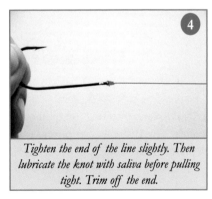

Tighten the end of the line slightly. Then lubricate the knot with saliva before pulling tight. Trim off the end.

Shockleader

A shockleader or leader as it's commonly known, is a length of heavier line with a much higher breaking strain, tied to the end of your mainline from your reel. The primary purpose of the leader is to take the strain off of the thinner mainline when casting, to avoid damaging or snapping the line. In such cases, you would need the half hitch and improved clinch knot shown below to attach the leader to the main line. You would then need to load 15-20 ft of leader onto your reel - this ensures you still have a few turns of leader on the spool of your reel when casting.

Half Hitch and Improved Clinch Knot

There are many different knots available for tying mono leader to mono mainline, however I find this is the simplest and easiest to make.

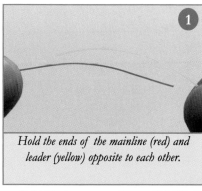

Hold the ends of the mainline (red) and leader (yellow) opposite to each other.

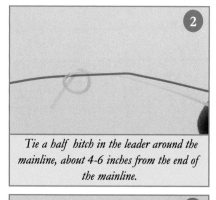

Tie a half hitch in the leader around the mainline, about 4-6 inches from the end of the mainline.

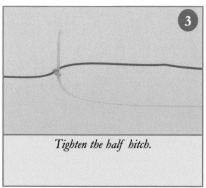

Tighten the half hitch.

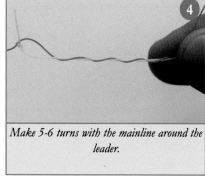

Make 5-6 turns with the mainline around the leader.

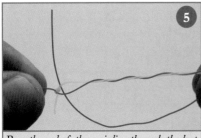

Run the end of the mainline through the loop created between the half hitch and mainline.

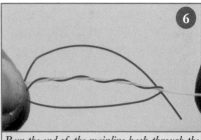

Run the end of the mainline back through the outside loop.

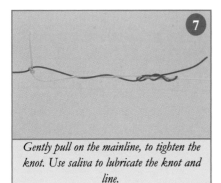

Gently pull on the mainline, to tighten the knot. Use saliva to lubricate the knot and line.

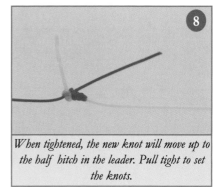

When tightened, the new knot will move up to the half hitch in the leader. Pull tight to set the knots.

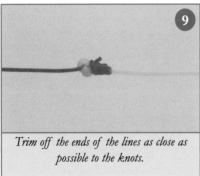
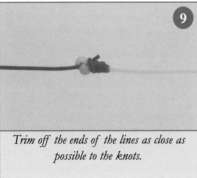

Trim off the ends of the lines as close as possible to the knots.

Improved Albright Special

Mono to Braid is always a tricky knot to figure out. The braid is so fine it can cut through the mono line very easily. This is a variation on the tried and

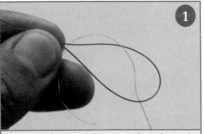

tested Albright knot, this one being a little more secure in my opinion. It is used for joining lines of different diameter and material and probably the best knot for tying braid to mono leader as it doesn't allow the braid to cut into the mono as some other knots do.

Make a loop in the mono (red) and run the braided mainline (green) through it and around the butt.

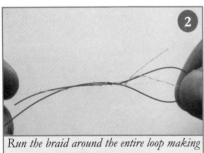

Run the braid around the entire loop making a total of 12 turns working towards the loop.

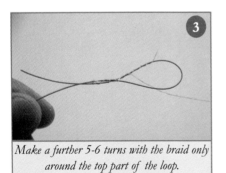

Make a further 5-6 turns with the braid only around the top part of the loop.

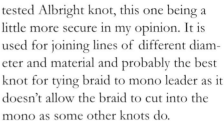

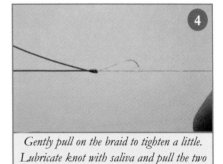

Gently pull on the braid to tighten a little. Lubricate knot with saliva and pull the two ends to tighten.

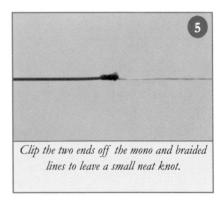

Clip the two ends off the mono and braided lines to leave a small neat knot.

Single Hook, Clipped Down Paternoster

This is one of the simplest and most commonly used rigs. The main components of the rig depend largely on the ground conditions and the species fish being sought. As a standard measure, when fishing clean ground the main line of the trace body should be at least 30lb clear mono, and in this case the hook length should be a minimum of 20lb clear mono. I would always use clear amnesia line for my trace bodies and hooklengths just in case the unusual colours of other lines might deter fish. The swivel at the top of the main trace should be a size 10 (69lb) rolling swivel and the swivel to which the hook length is attached should also be a size 10 rolling swivel. You can go smaller with the rolling swivels, a size 12 would be fine, however they are very small and difficult to handle. The hook size can vary according to the bait used and fish targeted. As a guide, a 2/0 hook should work in a lot of different situations. The same applies for the lead, and again, as a guide, in relatively mild conditions a 3-4oz grip lead should hold on a beach, but very often the grip is not necessary.

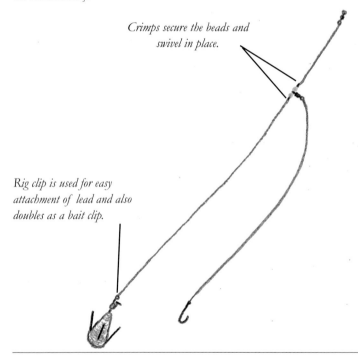

Crimps secure the beads and swivel in place.

Rig clip is used for easy attachment of lead and also doubles as a bait clip.

3 Hook Flapper

This is a standard competition rig that proves to probably be the most successful for catching higher quantities of fish. Its name comes from the amount of hooks on the trace and the fact that they flap in the wind when casted out. As there are 3 hooks used, more scent is released around the area. Also, it will catch bottom feeding fish and fish that are feeding higher up in the water. Its construction is very simple, again as standard measure, use 30lb clear amnesia mainline and 20lb hooklength, adjusting for ground conditions and species being sought. Use crimps to secure the beads on either side of the size 10 (69lb) rolling swivels leading to the hooklengths. On top of the trace use a size 10 rolling swivel also and at the bottom of the trace use a standard rig clip to attach the weight. Always ensure the hooklengths do not overlap on the next hooklength down the trace when hanging, as this will cause tangles. Again, the size of hook used will vary according to bait being used and species sought, however a size 2/0 hook will be suitable in most cases. The weight used will vary also according to weather conditions, tides and ground.

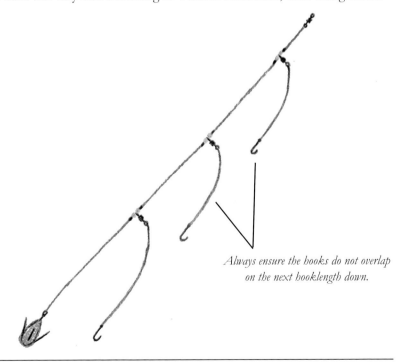

Always ensure the hooks do not overlap on the next hooklength down.

29

PEELER CRAB
Everything you need to know

Crabs inhabit our shoreline all year round and come in varying species and sizes. They are considered a nuisance by most anglers, as when casting out a perfect and well presented bait, it can be stripped from your hook in just a few minutes by the waiting hungry crab. This is certainly an annoyance for the angler; however, you can forgive the crab for the problems it creates in such situations, as, when the time is right, it will become the perfect bait itself, and in the eyes of many experienced anglers, the most successful bait they will use.

The common shore crab is an invertebrate, i.e. an animal without a backbone. Their outer shell has two main purposes; 1) as protection from predators and other potential enemies, and 2) as a support for the crab itself, as it does not have a backbone. However, unfortunately for the crab, but not for the angler and many species of fish, the shell is a fixed size and cannot grow. Therefore, as the crab itself grows inside, eventually, it will have to shed its old, small shell and grow a new one. This is the stage when the crab is at its most vulnerable, and is what we call the Peeler Stage or Moulting Stage. At this stage, the crab releases hormones or a scent that many believe can be tracked by a fish from up to a mile away.

The crab will start to grow a new shell underneath the outer shell and when it is ready, it will start to ingest a lot of water. Once enough water has been taken in by the crab, the force will push out on the old shell and cause it to crack. A lot of the time, you can see the cracks on the shell, usually starting at the lower back. Eventually the shell will crack and separate completely, leaving the crab defenceless with a soft skin-like outer shell. Over the next week, the crab will continue to ingest more water. This ensures that the new shell will be larger so once it hardens; the crab can expel the excess water and shrink back to its normal size, leaving a large shell in which it can grow for some time without having to moult continuously through its growth. Many crabs will moult up to 3 times a year, the majority moulting in certain areas around the country at specific times of the year. The times of moulting are determined by hormones and the environment in which the crab lives, so they do vary significantly. However, there are two very specific moults in many parts of Ireland, one around May and the other around September/October when peelers can be found in greater numbers.

Finding Peeler Crabs

This is an area in which the assistance of an experienced angler can be a great help to an inexperienced hand. A lot of anglers, when starting out, can be put off using peeler crab as they find them so difficult to locate. However, there

Along a stretch of weedy rocks on the coastline is always a good place to find peelers.

A great place to lay some traps is along mudflats in estuaries.

are some places that they will be in greater numbers. When the crab is going through the pre-moult stage; i.e. starting to grow its new shell under the old one, it seeks refuge away from predators, strong currents and crashing waves. Once it finds a suitable hiding place, it will stay there until its new shell is hard enough to allow it to become completely mobile again. Along the shoreline of the open sea, you can find peeler crabs under rocks and manmade traps such as cavity blocks and half pipes that would be otherwise submerged at high tide. Lifting or turning rocks at low tide will often reveal peelers. It is not good etiquette to search other people's traps and make sure to return any rocks to their original position to ensure preservation of the natural coastline and allow the rock to be inhabited by another crab at the moulting stage.

Identifying Peelers

The next step is to find out if the crab you have caught is indeed a peeler. There are many different ways of doing this, but the more experienced angler will know the minute they turn the rock. The old shell will apper duller in colour than normal. It may show cracks, usually at the lower back and sometimes the sides. These are indicators that the crab is well into the moulting stage, however, if the crab is only in the pre-moult stage, these signs will not be visible. Therefore, the most tried and tested method will be used. By

When the 1st segment of the back leg is removed, a replacement segment shows the crab is a peeler.

The crab is prime bait when the shell is actually lifting off at the back. This one is just popping.. perfect!

removing the first segment of one of the back legs, usually by gently twisting it, you can see if the crab is a peeler or not. If you are left with a white sinew, the crab is not a peeler; however, if you are left with a new, fleshy replacement segment, then the crab is a peeler.

Another good indicator of a peeler is when you find a large crab holding a smaller one underneath. This is actually a male crab holding the female underneath him waiting for her to moult. The reason for this is that females can only mate when they have moulted and are left with a soft shell. When a female is ready to moult, she sends out a distinctive scent to attract potential mates. When the 'first mate' arrives, he will often pull the female up underneath him to guard her from other potential mates. He will hold her until she moults and he can mate with her. I have met some anglers who prefer to use male peeler crabs rather than females, as they believe the scent of a female peeler used as bait will attract unwanted attention from male crabs. I have also met anglers who prefer to use the female as they release the 'attraction scent' that not only attracts male crabs but also fish, but I have failed to notice any difference myself. The male visually differs from the female in that his tail plate (the back part of the under body) is quite pointed while the female's plate will be more rounded.

Keeping Peeler crab

You need to keep the peeler crab in as good a state as possible. Therefore it is imperative that you store peelers in a fridge if possible, or similar conditions. The peeler can be kept in a container, and covered with either seaweed or a cloth, both soaked in fresh seawater. Some people also put a few millimetres of sea water into the container. It is an idea to put a lid on the container to prevent any of the livelier crabs from escaping, but if doing so, ensure that you make plenty of holes to allow the circulation of air. You should soak the seaweed or cloth with fresh seawater a few times a week to keep the crabs alive.

Keep the peeler crab in a container with a few millimeters of fresh seawater and cover with seaweed or a cloth.

Depending on when you plan to use the peeler crab, you can either slow down the moulting process or speed it up. If you keep the peelers at around 5 or 6 degrees, you can slow down the moulting; however, even a few degrees colder will almost halt it completely. If you wish to speed up the moulting process, you can add more fresh sea water to the container and move them to a warmer temperature. Sometimes you will see bubbles, as the crabs ingest more water.

Just before the crab sheds its old shell is widely regarded as the perfect stage of the peeling process for bait. This is when you should see a cracking of the shell, or the shell actually rising up off the back of the crab. At this stage the peeler will be almost lifeless and can be distinguished from the livelier ones in the earlier stage of the process. With time and experience you will be able to judge the speed of the moult against the date of your fishing trip to have your peelers at the perfect state when you need them.

Preparation

When preparing the crab for bait, many people prefer to kill the crab for humane reasons before removing the shell etc., while others will just kill it if they are cutting the bait in half once prepared. If you wish to kill the crab immediately, you can just stick a knife through the centre of the head, where the eyes are.

1. Peel the old back shell off where you will be left with a soft fleshy shell.

2. Remove the claws and legs by twisting them. If you rush this part too much, you may end up tearing half the body apart, so take your time. You can keep the legs and claws and remove their outer shells, as they also can be used as bait, or for tipping off the bait.

3. Remove the shell from the tail by flipping it down from the body and sliding it gently off. Also gently remove all hard shell areas in the middle body, the front mouth area and also just to the sides of the mouth.

4. Using your finger, push into the area of the mouth and you should see a white bone which you should remove.

5. On the sides of the peeler, you should see a group of brown fins, similar to the fins in a car radiator. These are the lungs and are also removed by most angers.

Presentation

Always ensure that you are using a hook size that will hold the size of the bait you are using, without compromising the tip of your hook. Many people will use only half a decent sized crab, but this will depend on the target species and target size.

Thread the hook though the leg sockets and out through the body. Using the leg sockets provides an added security to the bait on the hook, but is usually not enough to keep the bait on.

In most cases, the bait should be wrapped on the hook using elastic thread, as thin as possible. The idea here is to wrap the bait in enough thread to keep the bait on, but not too much, that it may deter fish.

Once the bait is on the hook, always ensure the hook tip is clear, or else you should pre-pare yourself for plenty of nibbles from fish but no take!

Of course not everyone has time to go out looking for peelers, let alone set traps for them. In some cases a trip is organised at the last minute and you have no time to collect bait. In these cases, the only way to get peeler crab is to take a trip to your local tackle shop or bait supplier. The bait is usually high quality and you can purchase crabs at the start of the peeling process for use at a later date or crabs just about to pop for immediate use. I must personally recommend Andrew Boyce's bait shop, in Shankill, Co Dublin, as his bait has been excellent every time. Contact information for Andrew: **Tel 085 1006207**

Rod Sutterby

COMMON SMOOTHHOUND
(Mustelus Mustelus)
By Cormac Walsh

The shifting sands of many of our beaches here in Ireland provide the sporting angler with an opportunity for fantastic fishing in the summer months, when the hordes of Smoothhound hit the shore. It can result in great craic and the best sport fishing on offer.

The Smoothhound is a sleek predator and miniature shark. It has two high dorsal fins. Its snout is gradually rounded with elongated and prominent nasal flaps, which are well separated from each other and the mouth. Its upper body is grey to pale brown, going to off-white on the underside. It is common throughout Irish waters and it can grow up to 25 lbs and is usually found over sand on shallow beaches. It offers great sport and lives up to its name with taking the bait fast and making hard runs.

Another species of Smoothhound, the Starry Smoothhound, is also caught occasionally but is less common in Irish waters. The main difference in appearance be seen by the white, starry spot markings above the dorsal line.

Rigs and Bait
Smoothhounds hit hard and fast therefore gear should be tough and rigs should be kept simple, clip down single hook or pennel pulley rigs up to 3ft, with up to 70lb body and 30lb snoods are ideal with a strong 3/ 0 hook at the

business end. Best baits are by far crab, either peeler or hardback. However, they won't turn their nose up at fish baits like fresh Mackerel and Sandeel. Ragworm and Lugworm can also be effective.

Tides and Times.

Late spring and right through to September are the peak months for Smoothhound. Fishing a small tide after a relatively settled period of mild weather and an onshore breeze can be productive.

Fishing from low water up to the top of the tide and an hour or so back. However I appreciate that each location is different. A lot of anglers have different thoughts on the time of day which is most productive with some swearing by daylight tides, especially dawn, coinciding with a high tide; and others preferring a night tide. Experimentation is your best bet and

Bruno Seifert with a Starry Smoothhound on Ballyhealy Beach, Co Wexford.

I have found a session at dawn with a hi-tide around 6/7am can have some great results as the hounds really switch on at first light.

Location

Smoothhound can be caught more or less anywhere on the Irish coast. If you want to increase your chances of catching a Smoothie the beaches of south Wicklow and east and south Wexford are among the most popular marks for fishing from the shore.

Smoothhounds hunt in packs and as a consequence, you can fish for hours without a bite, and then have an hour of frantic activity that stops in an instant. Large specimens hunt alone. They can attack your bait at any location when least expected, probably during a quiet calm session when a blank looks likely.

THE SOLUNAR THEORY

As I'm sure all anglers have experienced, on certain fishing trips there seems to be defined periods in which most fish are caught, usually within one hour. I have experienced this on numerous occasions, well, on trips where I have actually caught more than one fish! I never really thought about this over the years, usually attributing it to a shoal of fish or perhaps a turn of tide. However with the new digital age came a seemingly endless amount of information on the internet. I stumbled upon the theory behind these particular periods of peak activity some time ago, and as it turns out, this has been common knowledge for many anglers and hunters for a long time.

In 1926 John Alden Knight decided to investigate factors that might determine fish activity. Out of 33 possible influences, he narrowed it down to 3 main factors, sunrise/sunset, phase of the moon and the tides. From this, he created the Solunar Theory.

Tides and moon phases have long been associated with fish activity and fishing success. However Knight noted that there seemed to be more than just these factors influencing fish activity, as there were certain points during each day for one to two hours where most fish were caught. As his research continued, he determined that in addition to the time of moon up (directly overhead) and moon down (directly underfoot) there were intermediate periods of fishing activity that occurred midway between the two major periods which were at moon rise and moon set. So he coined the phrases 'major periods' when the moon is directly overhead or underneath and 'minor periods' when the moon rises and sets. The times of minor activity were not as successful as the times of major activity, but nevertheless some showed frenzied feeding and a definite increase in activity than the rest of the day. The major peaks lasted for up to two hours whereas the minor periods lasted for only one hour.

To back up this theory, Knight studied the timing of 200 'record' catches, and found that more than 90 percent were made during a new moon (when no moon is visible). This is the time when solunar periods appear strongest, and they were made during the actual times of the solunar periods.

During a full moon, the sun and moon are nearly opposite each other and given the length of the day, one or the other is nearly always above the horizon. During a new moon, both bodies are in near-perfect rhythm travelling the skies together with their forces combined. When a maximum solunar period falls within 30-60 minutes of sunrise or sunset, you can expect great activity and when this falls within the new moon (no moon) or full moon period, you can expect spectacular fishing.

Another thing to remember in dealing with solunar periods is that solunar influence will vary in intensity according to the position of the moon. The times of new moon (the dark of the moon), and full moon are the times of maximum intensity. Ocean tides reflect this intensity in their magnitude. This will last about three days, and wildlife will respond with maximum activity. Thereafter the degree of intensity tapers off until it is at its minimum during the third quarter phase of the moon.

Research has shown that a natural day for fish and many other animal species is based on a diurnal (twice daily) 'biological clock' that appears to coincide with lunar time. In other words it is based on the time that it takes the moon to complete one rotation of the earth (an average of 24 hours and 53 minutes). This is also called a 'tidal day' and explains why ocean tides are about an hour later each day - and why most fish, fresh water species included, will feed up to an hour later (in relation to our solar clock) each day.

Of course, local factors must be taken into account when fishing. If there are no fish in the area in which you are fishing, then you will obviously not catch anything regardless of whether or not it is a peak time in the solunar table. Weather conditions, pressure, tides, fish stocks, spawning and local environment usually dictate where fish will be at any point in time. These factors need to be taken into account before you even decide where you are going to fish. However, if you can find the fish, I hope the following solunar tables can help you all in your fishing experiences in 2009.

The tables listed over the next few pages show peak activity (Major and Minor) for each day of 2009. The calculations are based on Solar and Lunar times in Dublin; however the times can be adjusted slightly for your own area.

Times can be adjusted by 1 minute for every 12 miles, east and west of Dublin. For instance, if you are calculating times along the west coast of Ireland, you can add about 15 minutes to the Dublin time. If you are on the west coast of the UK you can subtract about 10 minutes from the Dublin time of if you are on the east coast of the UK you can subtract about 25 minutes from the Dublin Time.

Solunar Tables January 2009

- Date -		AM Minor	AM Major	PM Minor	PM Major	Sun Times Rises	Sun Times Sets	Moon Times Rises	Moon Times Sets	Moon Transit Up	Moon Transit Down
1	Thu		08:53	02:43	09:14	03:04	08:43	04:14	10:49a	9:56p	4:15p	3:54a
2	Fri		09:40	03:29	10:01	03:50	08:43		10:59a	11:11p	4:57p	4:36a
3	Sat	FQ	10:26	04:15	10:48	04:37	08:43	04:16	11:10a	xxxx	5:40p	5:18a
4	Sun		11:12	05:00	11:35	05:24	08:42	04:17	11:21a	12:29a	6:26p	6:02a
5	Mon		11:59	05:47	-----	06:12	08:42	04:18	11:35a	1:52a	7:16p	6:50a
6	Tue		12:21	06:35	12:49	07:03	08:42	04:20	11:53a	3:20a	8:10p	7:42a
7	Wed		01:12	07:27	01:43	07:58	08:41	04:21	12:20p	4:51a	9:11p	8:40a
8	Thu		02:07	08:23	02:39	08:55	08:41	04:22	1:02p	6:19a	10:15p	9:43a
9	Fri	*	03:06	09:23	03:39	09:56	08:40	04:24	2:05p	7:33a	11:21p	10:48a
10	Sat	*	04:08	10:24	04:40	10:57	08:39	04:25	3:27p	8:27a	xxxx	11:54a
11	Sun	FM*	05:11	11:27	05:42	11:57	08:39	04:27	5:02p	9:04a	12:26a	12:57p
12	Mon	*	06:14	12:00	06:42	12:28	08:38	04:28	6:38p	9:28a	1:28a	1:56p
13	Tue	*	07:14	01:01	07:40	01:27	08:37	04:30	8:10p	9:46a	2:24a	2:50p
14	Wed		08:11	01:59	08:35	02:23	08:36	04:32	9:36p	10:00a	3:15a	3:39p
15	Thu		09:04	02:53	09:27	03:15	08:35	04:33	10:57p	10:12a	4:03a	4:26p
16	Fri		09:54	03:43	10:16	04:05	08:34	04:35	xxxx	10:23a	4:48a	5:11p
17	Sat		10:41	04:30	11:04	04:53	08:33	04:37	12:17a	10:35a	5:33a	5:55p
18	Sun	LQ	11:27	05:16	11:50	05:39	08:32	04:38	1:36a	10:48a	6:18a	6:41p
19	Mon		-----	06:00	12:12	06:24	08:31	04:40	2:55a	11:05a	7:05a	7:28p
20	Tue		12:32	06:44	12:57	07:09	08:30	04:42	4:10a	11:28a	7:52a	8:17p
21	Wed		01:16	07:29	01:41	07:54	08:28	04:44	5:20a	11:59a	8:42a	9:07p
22	Thu		02:01	08:14	02:26	08:39	08:27	04:46	6:20a	12:43p	9:32a	9:57p
23	Fri		02:46	08:59	03:12	09:24	08:26	04:48	7:08a	1:39p	10:22a	10:47p
24	Sat	*	03:33	09:45	03:57	10:09	08:24	04:49	7:44a	2:45p	11:12a	11:36p
25	Sun	NM*	04:19	10:31	04:43	10:55	08:23	04:51	8:11a	3:59p	12:01p	xxxx
26	Mon	*	05:06	11:17	05:28	11:40	08:21	04:53	8:30a	5:15p	12:47p	12:24a
27	Tue	*	05:52	11:37	06:14	12:03	08:20	04:55	8:45a	6:31p	1:32p	1:10a
28	Wed	*	06:39	12:28	07:00	12:50	08:18	04:57	8:57a	7:47p	2:15p	1:54a
29	Thu		07:26	01:15	07:47	01:36	08:17	04:59	9:08a	9:02p	2:57p	2:36a
30	Fri		08:14	02:03	08:35	02:24	08:15	05:01	9:18a	10:18p	3:39p	3:18a
31	Sat		09:03	02:52	09:25	03:14	08:14	05:03	9:29a	11:37p	4:23p	4:01a

NM = New Moon	F Q = First Quarter Moon Phase * = Peak Activitiy
FM = Full Moon	L Q = Last Quarter Moon Phase

Solunar Tables February 2009

- Date -			AM		PM		Sun Times		Moon Times		Moon Transit	
			Minor	Major	Minor	Major	Rises	Sets	Rises	Sets	Up	Down
1	Sun		09:54	03:41	10:18	04:06	08:12	05:05	9:42a	xxxx	5:11p	4:47a
2	Mon	FQ	10:46	04:33	11:13	05:00	08:10	05:07	9:58a	1:01a	6:02p	5:36a
3	Tue		11:41	05:27	-----	05:56	08:08	05:09	10:21a	2:29a	6:58p	6:30a
4	Wed		12:08	06:23	12:38	06:54	08:07	05:11	10:55a	3:56a	7:59p	7:28a
5	Thu		01:04	07:20	01:36	07:52	08:05	05:13	11:47a	5:13a	9:03p	8:31a
6	Fri		02:01	08:17	02:33	08:49	08:03	05:15	12:59p	6:15a	10:07p	9:35a
7	Sat		02:59	09:14	03:30	09:45	08:01	05:17	2:26p	6:58a	11:09p	10:38a
8	Sun	*	03:55	10:10	04:24	10:39	07:59	05:19	4:01p	7:28a	xxxx	11:38a
9	Mon	*	04:50	11:04	05:17	11:31	07:57	05:21	5:35p	7:48a	12:07a	12:34p
10	Tue	FM*	05:44	11:57	06:09	-----	07:55	05:23	7:05p	8:04a	1:01a	1:26p
11	Wed	*	06:37	12:25	07:01	12:49	07:53	05:25	8:30p	8:17a	1:51a	2:15p
12	Thu	*	07:30	01:18	07:53	01:42	07:51	05:27	9:52p	8:29a	2:38a	3:01p
13	Fri		08:22	02:11	08:45	02:34	07:49	05:29	11:14p	8:41a	3:24a	3:47p
14	Sat		09:14	03:02	09:38	03:26	07:47	05:31	xxxx	8:54a	4:11a	4:34p
15	Sun		10:05	03:53	10:29	04:17	07:45	05:33	12:35a	9:10a	4:58a	5:22p
16	Mon		10:56	04:44	11:20	05:08	07:43	05:35	1:54a	9:31a	5:46a	6:11p
17	Tue	LQ	11:45	05:33	-----	05:58	07:41	05:37	3:07a	9:59a	6:36a	7:01p
18	Wed		12:08	06:21	12:33	06:46	07:39	05:39	4:11a	10:39a	7:26a	7:51p
19	Thu		12:55	07:07	01:20	07:32	07:37	05:41	5:04a	11:30a	8:16a	8:41p
20	Fri		01:40	07:52	02:05	08:17	07:35	05:43	5:44a	12:33p	9:06a	9:31p
21	Sat		02:24	08:36	02:48	09:00	07:32	05:45	6:13a	1:44p	9:55a	10:19p
22	Sun	*	03:07	09:19	03:30	09:42	07:30	05:47	6:35a	3:00p	10:43a	11:06p
23	Mon	*	03:49	10:01	04:12	10:23	07:28	05:49	6:51a	4:17p	11:28a	11:50p
24	Tue	NM*	04:32	10:42	04:53	11:04	07:26	05:51	7:05a	5:34p	12:12p	xxxx
25	Wed	*	05:15	11:00	05:36	-----	07:24	05:53	7:16a	6:50p	12:55p	12:34a
26	Thu	*	06:00	11:45	06:21	12:11	07:21	05:55	7:27a	8:06p	1:38p	1:17a
27	Fri	*	06:48	12:36	07:10	12:59	07:19	05:57	7:38a	9:25p	2:22p	2:00a
28	Sat		07:39	01:27	08:03	01:51	07:17	05:59	7:50a	10:48p	3:09p	2:45a

NM = New Moon	F Q = First Quarter Moon Phase	* = Peak Activitiy
FM = Full Moon	L Q = Last Quarter Moon Phase	

Solunar Tables

Solunar Tables March 2009

- Date -			AM		PM		Sun Times		Moon Times		Moon Transit	
			Minor	Major	Minor	Major	Rises	Sets	Rises	Sets	Up	Down
1	Sun		08:34	02:21	09:00	02:47	07:14	06:01	8:05a	xxxx	3:59p	3:33a
2	Mon		09:32	03:18	10:00	03:46	07:12	06:03	8:26a	12:15a	4:53p	4:25a
3	Tue	FQ	10:33	04:18	11:02	04:48	07:10	06:05	8:55a	1:41a	5:51p	5:22a
4	Wed		11:34	05:19	-----	05:50	07:08	06:07	9:40a	3:00a	6:52p	6:21a
5	Thu		12:03	06:19	12:34	06:50	07:05	06:08	10:43a	4:06a	7:54p	7:23a
6	Fri		01:01	07:16	01:31	07:46	07:03	06:10	12:03p	4:54a	8:55p	8:25a
7	Sat		01:55	08:10	02:24	08:39	07:01	06:12	1:33p	5:28a	9:53p	9:25a
8	Sun		02:46	09:00	03:13	09:27	06:58	06:14	3:05p	5:51a	10:48p	10:21a
9	Mon	*	03:34	09:47	04:00	10:12	06:56	06:16	4:35p	6:08a	xxxx	11:14a
10	Tue	*	04:21	10:33	04:45	10:57	06:53	06:18	6:01p	6:22a	11:39p	12:03p
11	Wed	FM*	05:09	11:00	05:32	11:20	06:51	06:20	7:24p	6:35a	12:27a	12:50p
12	Thu	*	05:58	11:46	06:21	12:09	06:49	06:21	8:47p	6:47a	1:14a	1:37p
13	Fri	*	06:49	12:37	07:13	01:01	06:46	06:23	10:09p	6:59a	2:00a	2:24p
14	Sat		07:42	01:30	08:07	01:55	06:44	06:25	xxxx	7:14a	2:48a	3:12p
15	Sun		08:37	02:25	09:02	02:50	06:42	06:27	11:31p	7:33a	3:37a	4:02p
16	Mon		09:32	03:19	09:57	03:45	06:39	06:29	12:48a	7:59a	4:27a	4:52p
17	Tue		10:26	04:13	10:51	04:39	06:37	06:30	1:58a	8:34a	5:17a	5:43p
18	Wed		11:00	05:06	11:18	05:31	06:34	06:32	2:55a	09:21a	6:08a	6:33p
19	Thu		11:43	05:55	12:08	06:20	06:32	06:34	3:40a	10:20a	6:58a	7:23p
20	Fri		12:30	06:42	12:54	07:06	06:30	06:36	4:14a	11:28a	7:48a	8:12p
21	Sat		01:14	07:26	01:37	07:49	06:27	06:38	4:38a	12:42p	8:36a	8:59p
22	Sun		01:56	08:07	02:18	08:30	06:25	06:39	4:56a	1:58p	9:22a	9:44p
23	Mon		02:35	08:46	02:57	09:08	06:22	06:41	5:11a	3:15p	10:06a	10:28p
24	Tue	*	03:14	09:25	03:36	09:47	06:20	06:43	5:23a	4:31p	10:50a	xxxx
25	Wed	*	03:54	10:05	04:16	10:27	06:18	06:45	5:34a	5:48p	11:33a	11:11p
26	Thu	NM*	04:36	10:48	04:59	11:10	06:15	06:47	5:45a	7:08p	12:17p	11:55p
27	Fri	*	05:23	11:11	05:47	11:35	06:13	06:48	5:58a	8:31p	1:04p	12:40a
28	Sat	*	06:15	12:02	06:41	12:28	06:10	06:50	6:12a	09:58p	1:54p	1:28a
29	Sun		08:13	01:59	08:41	02:27	07:08	07:52	7:31a	xxxx	3:48p	3:20a
30	Mon		09:16	03:01	09:46	03:31	07:06	07:54	7:58a	12:26a	4:45p	4:16a
31	Tue		10:22	04:07	10:52	04:37	07:03	07:55	8:38a	1:49a	5:46p	5:16a

NM = New Moon	F Q = First Quarter Moon Phase	* = Peak Activitiy
FM = Full Moon	L Q = Last Quarter Moon Phase	

44

Solunar Tables April 2009

- Date -			AM		PM		Sun Times		Moon Times		Moon Transit	
			Minor	Major	Minor	Major	Rises	Sets	Rises	Sets	Up	Down
1	Wed		11:28	05:12	11:58	05:43	07:01	07:57	9:35a	2:59a	6:48p	6:17a
2	Thu	FQ	12:06	06:15	12:30	06:45	06:58	07:59	10:50a	3:52a	7:48p	7:18a
3	Fri		12:59	07:14	01:28	07:42	06:56	08:01	12:15p	4:29a	8:46p	8:18a
4	Sat		01:53	08:06	02:20	08:33	06:54	08:02	1:45p	4:55a	9:41p	9:14a
5	Sun		02:41	08:53	03:06	09:19	06:51	08:04	3:14p	5:14a	10:31p	10:07a
6	Mon		03:25	09:36	03:48	10:00	06:49	08:06	4:39p	5:28a	11:19p	10:56a
7	Tue		04:06	10:18	04:29	10:41	06:47	08:08	6:01p	5:41a	xxxx	11:42a
8	Wed	*	04:48	11:00	05:11	11:23	06:44	08:10	7:22p	5:53a	12:05a	12:28p
9	Thu	*	05:33	11:45	05:56	-----	06:42	08:11	8:44p	6:05a	12:51a	1:14p
10	Fri	FM*	06:21	12:09	06:45	12:33	06:40	08:13	10:06p	6:19a	1:38a	2:02p
11	Sat	*	07:13	01:00	07:38	01:25	06:37	08:15	11:26p	6:36a	2:26a	2:51p
12	Sun	*	08:08	01:55	08:33	02:20	06:35	08:17	xxxx	6:59a	3:16a	3:42p
13	Mon		09:04	02:51	09:30	03:17	06:33	08:18	12:40a	7:30a	4:07a	4:33p
14	Tue		10:01	03:48	10:26	04:14	06:30	08:20	1:44a	8:13a	4:59a	5:24p
15	Wed		10:56	04:43	11:21	05:08	06:28	08:22	2:34a	9:08a	5:50a	6:15p
16	Thu		11:48	05:36	-----	06:00	06:26	08:24	3:12a	10:12a	6:40a	7:04p
17	Fri	LQ	12:13	06:25	12:37	06:49	06:24	08:26	3:40a	11:24a	7:28a	7:51p
18	Sat		12:59	07:11	01:22	07:33	06:21	08:27	4:00a	12:38p	8:14a	8:37p
19	Sun		01:42	07:53	02:03	08:14	06:19	08:29	4:16a	1:54p	8:59a	9:21p
20	Mon		02:21	08:32	02:42	08:53	06:17	08:31	4:29a	3:09p	9:42a	10:04p
21	Tue		02:58	09:09	03:20	09:31	06:15	08:33	4:40a	4:25p	10:25a	10:47p
22	Wed	*	03:36	09:47	03:59	10:10	06:13	08:35	4:52a	5:43p	11:09a	11:31p
23	Thu	*	04:17	10:28	04:40	10:52	06:11	08:36	5:04a	7:05p	11:54a	xxxx
24	Fri	NM*	05:02	11:15	05:27	11:40	06:08	08:38	5:17a	8:32p	12:44p	12:19a
25	Sat	*	05:53	-----	06:21	12:35	06:06	08:40	5:34a	10:03p	1:37p	1:10a
26	Sun	*	06:53	12:38	07:22	01:07	06:04	08:42	5:58a	11:31p	2:35p	2:05a
27	Mon	*	07:58	01:42	08:29	02:13	06:02	08:44	6:34a	xxxx	3:36p	3:05a
28	Tue		09:07	02:51	09:38	03:22	06:00	08:45	7:27a	12:48a	4:39p	4:08a
29	Wed		10:15	04:00	10:46	04:31	05:58	08:47	8:37a	1:48a	5:42p	5:11a
30	Thu		11:21	05:06	11:50	05:36	05:56	08:49	10:02a	2:31a	6:41p	6:12a

NM = New Moon	F Q = First Quarter Moon Phase	* = Peak Activitiy
FM = Full Moon	L Q = Last Quarter Moon Phase	

Solunar Tables May 2009

- Date -			AM		PM		Sun Times		Moon Times		Moon Transit	
			Minor	Major	Minor	Major	Rises	Sets	Rises	Sets	Up	Down
1	Fri	FQ	-----	06:07	12:20	06:34	05:54	08:51	11:31a	3:00a	7:37p	7:10a
2	Sat		12:47	07:00	01:13	07:25	05:52	08:53	1:00p	3:20a	8:28p	8:03a
3	Sun		01:35	07:47	01:58	08:10	05:50	08:54	2:25p	3:36a	9:16p	8:53a
4	Mon		02:17	08:28	02:40	08:51	05:48	08:56	3:46p	3:49a	10:02p	9:39a
5	Tue		02:56	09:08	03:19	09:30	05:46	08:58	5:06p	4:01a	10:47p	10:24a
6	Wed		03:36	09:47	03:59	10:10	05:44	09:00	6:26p	4:13a	11:32p	11:09a
7	Thu	*	04:17	10:29	04:41	10:52	05:42	09:01	7:46p	4:25a	xxxx	11:56a
8	Fri	*	05:02	11:14	05:26	11:39	05:41	09:03	9:06p	4:41a	12:19a	12:43p
9	Sat	FM*	05:51	-----	06:16	12:03	05:39	09:05	10:23p	5:01a	1:08a	1:33p
10	Sun	*	06:43	12:30	07:09	12:56	05:37	09:06	11:31p	5:29a	1:59a	2:24p
11	Mon	*	07:38	01:25	08:04	01:51	05:35	09:08	xxxx	6:07a	2:50a	3:16p
12	Tue		08:34	02:22	09:00	02:47	05:34	09:10	12:27a	6:58a	3:42a	4:07p
13	Wed		09:30	03:18	09:54	03:42	05:32	09:12	1:10a	7:59a	4:32a	4:57p
14	Thu		10:23	04:11	10:47	04:35	05:30	09:13	1:41a	9:08a	5:21a	5:45p
15	Fri		11:13	05:02	11:36	05:25	05:29	09:15	2:04a	10:21a	6:08a	6:31p
16	Sat	LQ	-----	05:49	12:00	06:11	05:27	09:16	2:21a	11:35a	6:53a	7:14p
17	Sun		12:20	06:33	12:44	06:54	05:26	09:18	2:35a	12:49p	7:36a	7:57p
18	Mon		01:03	07:14	01:24	07:35	05:24	09:20	2:47a	2:03p	8:18a	8:39p
19	Tue		01:42	07:53	02:04	08:14	05:23	09:21	2:58a	3:18p	9:00a	9:22p
20	Wed		02:20	08:32	02:43	08:54	05:21	09:23	3:09a	4:37p	9:44a	10:07p
21	Thu		03:00	09:13	03:25	09:37	05:20	09:24	3:22a	6:01p	10:31a	10:56p
22	Fri	*	03:45	09:58	04:12	10:25	05:18	09:26	3:37a	7:30p	11:22a	11:49p
23	Sat	*	04:35	10:50	05:05	11:20	05:17	09:27	3:58a	9:01p	12:18p	xxxx
24	Sun	NM*	05:34	11:49	06:05	12:21	05:16	09:29	4:28a	10:25p	1:19p	12:48a
25	Mon	*	06:38	12:22	07:11	12:54	05:15	09:30	5:13a	11:35p	2:23p	1:51a
26	Tue	*	07:47	01:31	08:19	02:03	05:14	09:31	6:18a	xxxx	3:28p	2:56a
27	Wed		08:57	02:41	09:28	03:12	05:12	09:33	7:41a	12:27a	4:31p	4:00a
28	Thu		10:03	03:49	10:32	04:18	05:11	09:34	9:12a	1:02a	5:30p	5:01a
29	Fri		11:04	04:51	11:31	05:18	05:10	09:35	10:44a	1:25a	6:25p	5:58a
30	Sat		11:59	05:46	-----	06:11	05:09	09:37	12:12p	1:43a	7:14p	6:50a
31	Sun	FQ	12:24	06:35	12:47	06:58	05:08	09:38	1:35p	1:57a	8:01p	7:38a

NM = New Moon	F Q = First Quarter Moon Phase	* = Peak Activitiy
FM = Full Moon	L Q = Last Quarter Moon Phase	

Solunar Tables June 2009

- Date -		AM		PM		Sun Times		Moon Times		Moon Transit	
		Minor	Major	Minor	Major	Rises	Sets	Rises	Sets	Up	Down
1	Mon		01:07	07:19	01:30	07:41	05:07	09:39	2:55p	2:09a	8:46p	8:23a
2	Tue		01:48	07:59	02:10	08:22	05:07	09:40	4:14p	2:21a	9:31p	9:08a
3	Wed		02:28	08:39	02:51	09:02	05:06	09:41	5:33p	2:34a	10:16p	9:53a
4	Thu		03:08	09:20	03:32	09:44	05:05	09:42	6:52p	2:48a	11:04p	10:40a
5	Fri		03:51	10:04	04:16	10:28	05:04	09:43	8:09p	3:06a	11:53p	11:28a
6	Sat	*	04:37	10:50	05:03	11:15	05:04	09:44	9:19p	3:31a	xxxx	12:19p
7	Sun	*	05:27	11:40	05:52	-----	05:03	09:45	10:19p	4:05a	12:44a	1:10p
8	Mon	FM*	06:18	12:06	06:44	12:31	05:03	09:46	11:07p	4:51a	1:35a	2:01p
9	Tue	*	07:12	12:59	07:36	01:24	05:02	09:47	11:42p	5:49a	2:26a	2:51p
10	Wed	*	08:05	01:53	08:29	02:17	05:02	09:48	xxxx	6:56a	3:16a	3:40p
11	Thu		08:57	02:45	09:20	03:08	05:01	09:48	12:08a	8:08a	4:04a	4:27p
12	Fri		09:47	03:36	10:08	03:58	05:01	09:49	12:27a	9:21a	4:49a	5:11p
13	Sat		10:34	04:24	10:55	04:45	05:01	09:50	12:42a	10:34a	5:32a	5:53p
14	Sun		11:19	05:09	11:40	05:30	05:01	09:50	12:54a	11:47a	6:14a	6:34p
15	Mon	LQ	-----	05:52	12:02	06:13	05:00	09:51	1:05a	12:59p	6:55a	7:15p
16	Tue		12:21	06:34	12:45	06:55	05:00	09:51	1:16a	2:14p	7:36a	7:58p
17	Wed		01:04	07:16	01:27	07:39	05:00	09:52	1:27a	3:33p	8:20a	8:44p
18	Thu		01:46	07:59	02:12	08:24	05:00	09:52	1:41a	4:57p	9:08a	9:34p
19	Fri		02:32	08:46	03:00	09:14	05:00	09:53	1:58a	6:26p	10:01a	10:29p
20	Sat		03:22	09:38	03:53	10:08	05:00	09:53	2:23a	7:54p	10:59a	11:30p
21	Sun	*	04:19	10:35	04:51	11:07	05:01	09:53	3:00a	9:13p	12:02p	xxxx
22	Mon	NM*	05:21	11:37	05:54	12:10	05:01	09:53	3:55a	10:14p	1:07p	12:34a
23	Tue	*	06:26	12:10	06:59	12:43	05:01	09:53	5:11a	10:57p	2:13p	1:40a
24	Wed	*	07:33	01:18	08:04	01:49	05:01	09:54	6:41a	11:27p	3:16p	2:45a
25	Thu	*	08:39	02:25	09:07	02:53	05:02	09:54	8:17a	11:47p	4:14p	3:45a
26	Fri		09:40	03:27	10:06	03:53	05:02	09:54	9:50a	xxxx	5:07p	4:41a
27	Sat		10:36	04:24	11:01	04:48	05:03	09:53	11:17a	12:03a	5:57p	5:32a
28	Sun		11:28	05:16	11:51	05:39	05:03	09:53	12:41p	12:17a	6:43p	6:20a
29	Mon	FQ	-----	06:04	12:15	06:27	05:04	09:53	2:02p	12:29a	7:29p	7:06a
30	Tue		12:37	06:48	01:00	07:11	05:04	09:53	3:22p	12:42a	8:15p	7:52a

NM = New Moon	F Q = First Quarter Moon Phase	* = Peak Activitiy
FM = Full Moon	L Q = Last Quarter Moon Phase	

Solunar Tables July 2009

- Date -			AM		PM		Sun Times		Moon Times		Moon Transit	
			Minor	Major	Minor	Major	Rises	Sets	Rises	Sets	Up	Down
1	Wed		01:20	07:31	01:43	07:55	05:05	09:53	4:41p	12:56a	9:02p	8:38a
2	Thu		02:02	08:14	02:27	08:39	05:06	09:52	5:58p	1:13a	9:51p	9:26a
3	Fri		02:46	08:58	03:11	09:23	05:06	09:52	7:10p	1:36a	10:41p	10:16a
4	Sat		03:31	09:43	03:56	10:09	05:07	09:51	8:13p	2:07a	11:31p	11:06a
5	Sun	*	04:17	10:30	04:43	10:55	05:08	09:51	9:04p	2:48a	xxxx	11:57a
6	Mon	*	05:05	11:18	05:30	11:43	05:09	09:50	9:43p	3:42a	12:22a	12:47p
7	Tue	FM*	05:54	-----	06:18	12:06	05:10	09:50	10:12p	4:46a	1:12a	1:36p
8	Wed	*	06:43	12:31	07:06	12:55	05:11	09:49	10:33p	5:57a	2:00a	2:24p
9	Thu	*	07:32	01:21	07:54	01:43	05:12	09:48	10:49p	7:10a	2:47a	3:09p
10	Fri		08:20	02:09	08:41	02:30	05:13	09:47	11:02p	8:24a	3:31a	3:52p
11	Sat		09:07	02:56	09:27	03:17	05:14	09:47	11:13p	9:36a	4:13a	4:33p
12	Sun		09:52	03:42	10:13	04:03	05:15	09:46	11:24p	10:47a	4:53a	5:14p
13	Mon		10:38	04:28	10:59	04:48	05:16	09:45	11:35p	12:00p	5:34a	5:55p
14	Tue	LQ	11:24	05:13	11:46	05:35	05:18	09:44	11:47p	1:15p	6:16a	6:38p
15	Wed		-----	05:58	12:10	06:22	05:19	09:43	xxxx	2:34p	7:01a	7:24p
16	Thu		12:33	06:46	12:59	07:12	05:20	09:42	12:02a	3:58p	7:49a	8:16p
17	Fri		01:22	07:36	01:50	08:05	05:21	09:40	12:23a	5:24p	8:43a	9:12p
18	Sat		02:14	08:29	02:45	09:00	05:23	09:39	12:52a	6:46p	9:42a	10:13p
19	Sun		03:09	09:25	03:42	09:58	05:24	09:38	1:37a	7:55p	10:45a	11:18p
20	Mon	*	04:08	10:24	04:41	10:57	05:25	09:37	2:42a	8:47p	11:50a	xxxx
21	Tue	*	05:09	11:25	05:40	11:56	05:27	09:36	4:05a	9:23p	12:55p	12:23a
22	Wed	NM*	06:10	-----	06:40	12:55	05:28	09:34	5:39a	9:49p	1:56p	1:26a
23	Thu	*	07:11	12:57	07:39	01:25	05:30	09:33	7:16a	10:07p	2:53p	2:25a
24	Fri	*	08:10	01:57	08:36	02:23	05:31	09:31	8:48a	10:22p	3:46p	3:20a
25	Sat		09:07	02:55	09:31	03:19	05:33	09:30	10:16a	10:36p	4:35p	4:11a
26	Sun		10:01	03:49	10:25	04:13	05:34	09:28	11:41a	10:49p	5:23p	4:59a
27	Mon		10:53	04:41	11:17	05:05	05:36	09:27	1:04p	11:03p	6:10p	5:47a
28	Tue		11:44	05:32	-----	05:56	05:37	09:25	2:26p	11:19p	6:58p	6:34a
29	Wed	FQ	12:08	06:20	12:32	06:44	05:39	09:24	3:46p	11:40p	7:47p	7:23a
30	Thu		12:54	07:07	01:19	07:32	05:40	09:22	5:00p	xxxx	8:37p	8:12a
31	Fri		01:41	07:53	02:06	08:19	05:42	09:20	6:06p	12:09a	9:28p	9:03a

NM = New Moon	F Q = First Quarter Moon Phase	* = Peak Activitiy
FM = Full Moon	L Q = Last Quarter Moon Phase	

Solunar Tables August 2009

- Date -		AM		PM		Sun Times		Moon Times		Moon Transit	
		Minor	Major	Minor	Major	Rises	Sets	Rises	Sets	Up	Down
1	Sat		02:26	08:39	02:51	09:04	05:44	09:19	7:01p	12:47a	10:18p	9:53a
2	Sun		03:11	09:24	03:36	09:49	05:45	09:17	7:43p	1:37a	11:08p	10:44a
3	Mon		03:56	10:09	04:21	10:33	05:47	09:15	8:15p	2:38a	11:57p	11:33a
4	Tue	*	04:41	10:53	05:05	11:16	05:49	09:13	8:38p	3:47a	xxxx	12:21p
5	Wed	*	05:26	11:37	05:48	11:59	05:50	09:12	8:56p	4:59a	12:44a	1:07p
6	Thu	FM*	06:10	-----	06:31	12:21	05:52	09:10	9:10p	6:13a	1:29a	1:51p
7	Fri	*	06:54	12:44	07:15	01:05	05:54	09:08	9:22p	7:26a	2:12a	2:33p
8	Sat	*	07:39	01:29	08:00	01:50	05:55	09:06	9:33p	8:39a	2:53a	3:14p
9	Sun		08:25	02:15	08:46	02:35	05:57	09:04	9:44p	9:50a	3:34a	3:55p
10	Mon		09:12	03:02	09:34	03:23	05:59	09:02	9:56p	11:04a	4:15a	4:37p
11	Tue		10:02	03:50	10:24	04:13	06:00	09:00	10:09p	12:21p	4:59a	5:21p
12	Wed		10:53	04:41	11:18	05:05	06:02	08:58	10:27p	1:41p	5:45a	6:10p
13	Thu	LQ	11:47	05:33	-----	06:00	06:04	08:56	10:52p	3:04p	6:35a	7:02p
14	Fri		12:18	06:28	12:42	06:57	06:05	08:54	11:29p	4:25p	7:31a	8:00p
15	Sat		01:08	07:24	01:39	07:54	06:07	08:52	xxxx	5:38p	8:30a	9:01p
16	Sun		02:05	08:21	02:36	08:52	06:09	08:50	12:23a	6:36p	9:32a	10:03p
17	Mon		03:01	09:17	03:33	09:48	06:11	08:48	1:36a	7:18p	10:35a	11:06p
18	Tue		03:57	10:12	04:27	10:42	06:12	08:46	3:04a	7:47p	11:37a	xxxx
19	Wed	*	04:52	11:06	05:20	11:35	06:14	08:43	4:38a	8:09p	12:35p	12:06a
20	Thu	NM*	05:46	11:59	06:13	12:26	06:16	08:41	6:13a	8:26p	1:30p	1:03a
21	Fri	*	06:40	12:27	07:05	12:53	06:17	08:39	7:43a	8:40p	2:22p	1:56a
22	Sat	*	07:34	01:22	07:59	01:47	06:19	08:37	9:11a	8:54p	3:11p	2:46a
23	Sun	*	08:29	02:17	08:54	02:42	06:21	08:35	10:37a	9:08p	4:00p	3:35a
24	Mon		09:25	03:12	09:50	03:37	06:23	08:32	12:02p	9:24p	4:49p	4:24a
25	Tue		10:20	04:07	10:45	04:33	06:24	08:30	1:25p	9:44p	5:39p	5:14a
26	Wed		11:14	05:01	11:40	05:27	06:26	08:28	2:44p	10:10p	6:30p	6:05a
27	Thu		-----	05:54	12:06	06:19	06:28	08:26	3:55p	10:45p	7:22p	6:56a
28	Fri	FQ*	12:31	06:44	12:57	07:09	06:29	08:23	4:54p	11:32p	8:13p	7:48a
29	Sat		01:19	07:32	01:44	07:57	06:31	08:21	5:41p	xxxx	9:04p	8:39a
30	Sun		02:05	08:17	02:30	08:42	06:33	08:19	6:16p	12:29a	9:53p	9:28a
31	Mon		02:49	09:01	03:12	09:24	06:35	08:16	6:42p	1:35a	10:40p	10:17a

NM = New Moon	F Q = First Quarter Moon Phase	* = Peak Activitiy
FM = Full Moon	L Q = Last Quarter Moon Phase	

Solunar Tables September 2009

- Date -			AM		PM		Sun Times		Moon Times		Moon Transit	
			Minor	Major	Minor	Major	Rises	Sets	Rises	Sets	Up	Down
1	Tue		03:31	09:42	03:53	10:05	06:36	08:14	7:02p	2:47a	11:26p	11:03a
2	Wed	*	04:11	10:22	04:33	10:44	06:38	08:12	7:17p	4:00a	xxxx	11:48a
3	Thu	*	04:51	11:02	05:12	11:23	06:40	08:09	7:30p	5:14a	12:09a	12:31p
4	Fri	FM*	05:32	11:42	05:53	-----	06:41	08:07	7:41p	6:27a	12:52a	1:12p
5	Sat	*	06:14	12:04	06:35	12:25	06:43	08:05	7:52p	7:40a	1:33a	1:54p
6	Sun	*	06:59	12:48	07:20	01:10	06:45	08:02	8:04p	8:53a	2:15a	2:36p
7	Mon		07:47	01:36	08:10	01:58	06:46	08:00	8:18p	10:10a	2:58a	3:20p
8	Tue		08:39	02:27	09:04	02:51	06:48	07:58	8:34p	11:29a	3:43a	4:07p
9	Wed		09:35	03:22	10:01	03:48	06:50	07:55	8:57p	12:51p	4:33a	4:59p
10	Thu		10:34	04:20	11:02	04:48	06:52	07:53	9:29p	2:12p	5:26a	5:54p
11	Fri	LQ	11:34	05:19	-----	05:49	06:53	07:50	10:16p	3:26p	6:23a	6:52p
12	Sat		12:11	06:19	12:35	06:50	06:55	07:48	11:20p	4:28p	7:22a	7:53p
13	Sun		01:03	07:18	01:33	07:48	06:57	07:46	xxxx	5:14p	8:23a	8:53p
14	Mon		01:58	08:13	02:28	08:43	06:58	07:43	12:40a	5:47p	9:23a	9:53p
15	Tue		02:51	09:05	03:19	09:33	07:00	07:41	2:09a	6:11p	10:21a	10:49p
16	Wed		03:40	09:54	04:07	10:20	07:02	07:38	3:41a	6:29p	11:16a	11:43p
17	Thu	*	04:28	10:41	04:53	11:06	07:03	07:36	5:12a	6:44p	12:08p	xxxx
18	Fri	*	05:16	11:28	05:40	11:52	07:05	07:33	6:40a	6:58p	12:58p	12:33a
19	Sat	NM*	06:05	-----	06:30	12:42	07:07	07:31	8:06a	7:12p	1:47p	1:22a
20	Sun	*	06:58	12:45	07:23	01:10	07:08	07:29	9:32a	7:27p	2:36p	2:12a
21	Mon	*	07:53	01:40	08:19	02:06	07:10	07:26	10:57a	7:46p	3:27p	3:02a
22	Tue		08:51	02:38	09:17	03:04	07:12	07:24	12:20p	8:10p	4:19p	3:53a
23	Wed		09:49	03:36	10:15	04:02	07:13	07:21	1:37p	8:42p	5:12p	4:45a
24	Thu		10:46	04:33	11:12	04:59	07:15	07:19	2:43p	9:25p	6:04p	5:38a
25	Fri		11:40	05:27	-----	05:53	07:17	07:17	3:35p	10:19p	6:56p	6:30a
26	Sat	FQ	12:07	06:19	12:31	06:43	07:19	07:14	4:15p	11:22p	7:46p	7:21a
27	Sun		12:54	07:06	01:18	07:30	07:20	07:12	4:44p	xxxx	8:34p	8:11a
28	Mon		01:39	07:50	02:02	08:13	07:22	07:09	5:06p	12:32a	9:21p	8:58a
29	Tue		02:20	08:31	02:42	08:53	07:24	07:07	5:23p	1:45a	10:05p	9:43a
30	Wed		02:58	09:09	03:19	09:30	07:26	07:04	5:36p	2:58a	10:47p	10:26a

NM = New Moon	F Q = First Quarter Moon Phase	* = Peak Activitiy
FM = Full Moon	L Q = Last Quarter Moon Phase	

Solunar Tables October 2009

- Date -		AM		PM		Sun Times		Moon Times		Moon Transit	
		Minor	Major	Minor	Major	Rises	Sets	Rises	Sets	Up	Down
1 Thu		03:35	09:46	03:56	10:07	07:27	07:02	5:48p	4:11a	11:29p	11:08a
2 Fri	*	04:13	10:23	04:34	10:44	07:29	07:00	6:00p	5:24a	xxxx	11:50a
3 Sat	*	04:52	11:03	05:14	11:24	07:31	06:57	6:12p	6:38a	12:11a	12:32p
4 Sun	FM*	05:35	11:47	05:58	-----	07:32	06:55	6:25p	7:54a	12:54a	1:16p
5 Mon	*	06:23	12:11	06:48	12:35	07:34	06:52	6:41p	9:14a	1:39a	2:03p
6 Tue	*	07:17	01:04	07:43	01:30	07:36	06:50	7:01p	10:37a	2:28a	2:54p
7 Wed		08:16	02:02	08:44	02:30	07:38	06:48	7:31p	12:00p	3:21a	3:49p
8 Thu		09:19	03:04	09:48	03:34	07:40	06:45	8:14p	1:17p	4:17a	4:47p
9 Fri		10:24	04:09	10:54	04:39	07:41	06:43	9:12p	2:22p	5:17a	5:47p
10 Sat		11:28	05:13	11:58	05:43	07:43	06:41	10:27p	3:12p	6:17a	6:47p
11 Sun	LQ	12:04	06:14	12:28	06:43	07:45	06:38	11:52p	3:49p	7:17a	7:46p
12 Mon		12:56	07:10	01:23	07:37	07:47	06:36	xxxx	4:15p	8:14a	8:42p
13 Tue		01:47	08:00	02:13	08:26	07:49	06:34	1:21a	4:34p	9:09a	9:35p
14 Wed		02:33	08:46	02:58	09:10	07:50	06:31	2:50a	4:50p	10:00a	10:25p
15 Thu		03:16	09:28	03:41	09:53	07:52	06:29	4:16a	5:04p	10:49a	11:13p
16 Fri		03:59	10:11	04:23	10:35	07:54	06:27	5:40a	5:18p	11:37a	xxxx
17 Sat	*	04:44	10:56	05:08	11:21	07:56	06:25	7:04a	5:32p	12:25p	xxxx
18 Sun	NM*	05:32	11:45	05:58	12:10	07:58	06:22	8:29a	5:49p	1:15p	12:50a
19 Mon	*	06:25	12:12	06:51	12:38	08:00	06:20	9:53a	6:10p	2:06p	1:41a
20 Tue	*	07:22	01:08	07:48	01:35	08:02	06:18	11:14a	6:38p	2:59p	2:33a
21 Wed	*	08:20	02:07	08:47	02:34	08:03	06:16	12:25p	7:17p	3:53p	3:26a
22 Thu		09:19	03:06	09:45	03:32	08:05	06:13	1:25p	8:07p	4:46p	4:19a
23 Fri		10:16	04:03	10:41	04:29	08:07	06:11	2:10p	9:08p	5:37p	5:12a
24 Sat		11:10	04:57	11:34	05:22	08:09	06:09	2:44p	10:16p	6:27p	6:02a
25 Sun		10:59	04:48	11:00	05:11	07:11	05:07	2:09p	10:28p	6:14p	5:51a
26 Mon	FQ	11:21	05:34	11:45	05:56	07:13	05:05	2:28p	xxxx	6:59p	6:37a
27 Tue		12:05	06:16	12:26	06:37	07:15	05:03	2:42p	11:41p	7:42p	7:20a
28 Wed		12:44	06:54	01:05	07:15	07:17	05:01	2:55p	12:53a	9:23p	8:02a
29 Thu		01:20	07:31	01:41	07:51	07:19	04:59	3:06p	2:05a	09:04p	8:44a
30 Fri		01:57	08:07	02:18	08:28	07:21	04:56	3:18p	3:18a	09:47p	09:25a
31 Sat		02:34	08:45	02:57	09:08	07:23	04:54	3:31p	4:33a	10:31p	10:09a

NM = New Moon	F Q = First Quarter Moon Phase	* = Peak Activitiy
FM = Full Moon	L Q = Last Quarter Moon Phase	

Solunar Tables November 2009

- Date -			AM		PM		Sun Times		Moon Times		Moon Transit	
			Minor	Major	Minor	Major	Rises	Sets	Rises	Sets	Up	Down
1	Sun	*	03:15	09:27	03:40	09:52	07:25	04:52	3:45p	5:51a	xxxx	10:55a
2	Mon	FM*	04:02	10:15	04:28	10:41	07:27	04:50	4:04p	7:14a	xxxx	11:45a
3	Tue	*	04:56	11:10	05:24	11:38	07:29	04:49	4:31p	8:39a	12:12a	12:39p
4	Wed	*	05:56	-----	06:26	12:11	07:31	04:47	5:09p	10:01a	1:08a	1:37p
5	Thu	*	07:01	12:46	07:32	01:17	07:33	04:45	6:04p	11:13a	2:08a	2:38p
6	Fri		08:09	01:54	08:40	02:24	07:34	04:43	7:15p	12:09p	3:09a	3:40p
7	Sat		09:16	03:01	09:45	03:30	07:36	04:41	8:38p	12:50p	4:10a	4:40p
8	Sun		10:18	04:04	10:46	04:32	07:38	04:39	10:07p	1:19p	5:09a	5:37p
9	Mon	LQ	11:15	05:02	11:41	05:28	07:40	04:37	11:35p	1:41p	6:05a	6:31p
10	Tue		-----	05:53	12:05	06:18	07:42	04:36	xxxx	1:57p	6:57a	7:21p
11	Wed		12:27	06:39	12:50	07:02	07:44	04:34	1:01a	2:11p	7:45a	8:09p
12	Thu		01:09	07:21	01:32	07:44	07:46	04:32	2:24a	2:25p	8:33a	8:56p
13	Fri		01:50	08:02	02:13	08:25	07:48	04:31	3:46a	2:38p	9:20a	9:43p
14	Sat		02:32	08:44	02:56	09:08	07:50	04:29	5:08a	2:54p	10:08a	10:32p
15	Sun	*	03:17	09:29	03:42	09:55	07:52	04:28	6:31a	3:13p	10:57a	11:23p
16	Mon	*	04:06	10:19	04:32	10:45	07:54	04:26	7:52a	3:38p	11:49a	xxxx
17	Tue	NM*	04:59	11:12	05:26	11:39	07:56	04:25	9:07a	4:12p	12:42p	12:15a
18	Wed	*	05:55	11:37	06:21	12:08	07:58	04:23	10:12a	4:57p	1:35p	1:09a
19	Thu	*	06:52	12:39	07:18	01:05	07:59	04:22	11:04a	5:54p	2:28p	2:02a
20	Fri		07:48	01:36	08:13	02:01	08:01	04:20	11:42a	7:00p	3:19p	2:54a
21	Sat		08:43	02:31	09:06	02:54	08:03	04:19	12:11p	8:11p	4:07p	3:43a
22	Sun		09:34	03:22	09:56	03:45	08:05	04:18	12:32p	9:24p	4:53p	4:30a
23	Mon		10:21	04:10	10:42	04:32	08:07	04:17	12:48p	10:36p	5:36p	5:15a
24	Tue	FQ	11:05	04:54	11:25	05:15	08:08	04:15	1:01p	11:47p	6:18p	5:57a
25	Wed		11:45	05:35	-----	05:56	08:10	04:14	1:13p	xxxx	6:58p	6:38a
26	Thu		12:04	06:14	12:24	06:34	08:12	04:13	1:24p	12:58a	7:39p	7:19a
27	Fri		12:41	06:52	01:02	07:13	08:14	04:12	1:36p	2:10a	8:22p	8:00a
28	Sat		01:19	07:31	01:42	07:54	08:15	04:11	1:50p	3:26a	9:08p	8:45a
29	Sun		02:00	08:13	02:25	08:38	08:17	04:10	2:07p	4:46a	9:58p	9:32a
30	Mon	*	02:46	09:00	03:14	09:27	08:18	04:09	2:30p	6:10a	10:53p	10:25a

NM = New Moon	F Q = First Quarter Moon Phase	* = Peak Activitiy
FM = Full Moon	L Q = Last Quarter Moon Phase	

Solunar Tables December 2009

- Date -			AM		PM		Sun Times		Moon Times		Moon Transit	
			Minor	Major	Minor	Major	Rises	Sets	Rises	Sets	Up	Down
1	Tue	*	03:38	09:53	04:08	10:23	08:20	04:09	3:03p	7:35a	11:52p	11:22a
2	Wed	FM*	04:37	10:53	05:08	11:24	08:21	04:08	3:51p	8:53a	xxxx	12:23p
3	Thu	*	05:42	11:57	06:13	-----	08:23	04:07	4:57p	9:58a	12:54a	1:26p
4	Fri	*	06:49	12:33	07:20	01:04	08:24	04:06	6:18p	10:47a	1:58a	2:29p
5	Sat		07:56	01:41	08:26	02:11	08:26	04:06	7:48p	11:21a	2:59a	3:29p
6	Sun		09:00	02:46	09:28	03:14	08:27	04:05	9:19p	11:46a	3:58a	4:26p
7	Mon		09:59	03:46	10:25	04:12	08:28	04:05	10:47p	12:04p	4:52a	5:18p
8	Tue		10:52	04:40	11:16	05:04	08:30	04:05	xxxx	12:19p	5:43a	6:07p
9	Wed	LQ	11:40	05:28	-----	05:52	08:31	04:04	12:12a	12:33p	6:31a	6:54p
10	Thu		12:01	06:13	12:24	06:36	08:32	04:04	1:34a	12:47p	7:18a	7:41p
11	Fri		12:43	06:55	01:07	07:19	08:33	04:04	2:55a	1:01p	8:05a	8:29p
12	Sat		01:26	07:38	01:50	08:03	08:34	04:03	4:17a	1:19p	8:53a	9:18p
13	Sun		02:10	08:23	02:35	08:48	08:35	04:03	5:37a	1:41p	9:43a	10:09p
14	Mon		02:56	09:09	03:22	09:35	08:36	04:03	6:53a	2:11p	10:35a	11:01p
15	Tue	*	03:45	09:59	04:12	10:25	08:37	04:03	8:01a	2:52p	11:28a	11:54p
16	Wed	NM*	04:37	10:50	05:03	11:16	08:38	04:03	8:57a	3:45p	12:20p	xxxx
17	Thu	*	05:30	11:13	05:55	-----	08:39	04:04	9:40a	4:47p	1:12p	12:46a
18	Fri	*	06:22	12:10	06:47	12:35	08:39	04:04	10:12a	5:57p	2:01p	1:37a
19	Sat	*	07:14	01:03	07:37	01:26	08:40	04:04	10:36a	7:09p	2:48p	2:25a
20	Sun		08:04	01:54	08:26	02:15	08:41	04:04	10:54a	8:21p	3:32p	3:10a
21	Mon		08:52	02:42	09:13	03:02	08:41	04:05	11:08a	9:32p	4:14p	3:53a
22	Tue		09:37	03:27	09:58	03:48	08:42	04:05	11:20a	10:42p	4:55p	4:35a
23	Wed		10:21	04:11	10:41	04:31	08:42	04:06	11:32a	11:53p	5:35p	5:15a
24	Thu	FQ	11:03	04:53	11:24	05:13	08:42	04:06	11:43a	xxxx	6:16p	5:55a
25	Fri		11:45	05:34	-----	05:56	08:43	04:07	11:56a	1:05a	6:59p	6:37a
26	Sat		12:04	06:16	12:28	06:40	08:43	04:08	12:10p	2:21a	7:46p	7:22a
27	Sun		12:48	07:01	01:14	07:27	08:43	04:09	12:30p	3:41a	8:37p	8:11a
28	Mon		01:35	07:49	02:03	08:17	08:43	04:09	12:57p	5:04a	9:33p	9:05a
29	Tue		02:26	08:41	02:57	09:12	08:43	04:10	1:37p	6:26a	10:34p	10:03a
30	Wed	*	03:23	09:39	03:54	10:10	08:43	04:11	2:34p	7:38a	11:38p	11:06a
31	Thu	*	04:24	10:40	04:55	11:11	08:43	04:12	3:49p	8:35a	xxxx	12:10p

NM = New Moon   F Q = First Quarter Moon Phase   * = Peak Activitiy

FM = Full Moon   L Q = Last Quarter Moon Phase

FISHING FOR INFORMATION ON THE INTERNET? THIS SITE HAS IT ALL.

Sea-Angling-Ireland.org
By Kieran Hanrahan

The website www.sea-angling-ireland.org started as a case study for work in 1998 when I was asked to build a content rich website. Co-founded with John Diamond, it has been added to over the years but the community forums added in 2003 really pushed it to the fore in Irish angling websites, with over a thousand people on it every day now. Most are home grown but in summer around 10% are tourists planning their fishing expeditions. We have added similar forums for pike, coarse and game angling and other innovations like a wiki whereby members can post articles.

Jim Hendricks and well known fishing guides and authors have kindly contributed superb articles, all available free of charge. We have resisted the temptation to commercialise the site - everything is available free of charge and it is open to anyone. All are welcome. As people get to know each other, this quality information about marks is passed privately between members using private messaging. For example, you might arrange to meet people first, fish with them a few times and then as people see each other's commitment to conservation, information on marks is exchanged. And there is a ton of information now collected on the site about tactics, methods, review of tackle and rods, competitions results, forthcoming open competitions... in short everything to do with sea angling in Ireland. We are in discussion with various parties about developing it further without losing the voluntary ethos. A massive amount of work is done by moderators and others, all free.

Sea Angling Ireland SAC

The first Internet based sea angling club emerged on the site three years ago and it is now one of the biggest in Ireland, with almost 100 members scattered across the island. Affiliated to the IFSA, it runs boat and shore master angler competitions as well as more informal meets.

The big difference to other clubs is that we are not restricted to fishing our competitions in one province only. In scheduling our competitions and events we look for the best marks on an island of Ireland basis given the time of year, thereby offering members a unique opportunity. Sharing information, experienced anglers helping new members, and people returning to the sport after many years, informs the club's approach - that and the "social" scene close to competition venues!

We hit Kerry for autumn Bass, east Cork for Painted Ray, Galway and Mayo for Thornbacks and specimen Dabs, Donegal for flatfish and Tope, Clare for Blue sharks, Galway for Porbeagles and Spurdogs, Waterford for Cod and Ling off the wrecks, Wexford for Smoothhounds, Bass and Flounder, and Northern Ireland for colder water species like Cuckoo Rays and proper Cod.

This year the lads are running a last man standing competition and there is even talk of running a pair's competition on the Aran Islands! There are no big cash prizes because this is a social club where the bragging rights and up to four places in the IFSA Master Angler competitions are the real prizes. We ran our first ever IFSA affiliated open competition this year and expect to repeat it next year. Despite a gale on mid summers day (yes!) for the five hours of the competition, it was well organised and praised by the competitors. Our membership is typically open around November each year and closes shortly into each new year. You can be a member here as well as in another IFSA affiliated club.

For more information on joining Sea Angling Ireland Sea Angling Club (SAISAC) please visit www.sea-angling-ireland.org.

BASS FISHING IN DUNGARVAN, CO WATERFORD

Dungarvan has long been considered the 'tourism capital of County Waterford'. It is a bustling little town and each year is host to many tourists from all over the world. Although there is some dispute about a monastic and early Viking settlement, the town owes its foundation to the Anglo-Normans in the 12th century. Their motte and bailey at Gallows Hill to the west of the town still stands today. Present day Dungarvan is a thriving commercial and tourist town and is a convenient location to stay for touring the Comeragh Mountains and the Ring Peninsula.

I first came across Arthur Daly in the angling forums on Sea-Angling-Ireland.org. He caught my attention immediately. He had started a discussion about predictable fishing, and at the time, I was working on my Solunar Theory article.

Arthur was telling other anglers when he was going fishing, approximately what time he would catch the fish, and how many he would catch! I know many anglers thought, what a load of rubbish, there's no way anyone can make those sort of predictions. But I believed him. He had explained the theory behind his predictions - the solunar theory, of which I was a firm believer.

I asked Arthur if he would be interested in taking me fishing in the Cunnigar, in Dungarvan with him sometime, so I could write an article about it. He

agreed and told me he would wait for the right tides and weather and give me a call. Growing up in Kilmore, in Co Wexford, I believe I actually have Bass fishing in my blood. It's like a natural instinct to go Bass fishing, it never leaves my mind. Arthur's reports stated that he will go out most days and catch an average of 8 Bass in a day. This is not something that I or most other anglers are used to. I couldn't wait for a call from him, and after tormenting myself for a couple weeks drawing blanks on several occasions, he finally called and invited me down for a session.

The wind had been coming from the northwest for a few days previously and the trusty weatherman in Met Eireann had confirmed that it would change overnight to a south westerly breeze. Of course the wind never came around to the south west for us. Arthur explained to me that the prevailing south to south-westerly wind not only brings a little stir into the water in Dungarvan, but as it is the prevailing wind, the fish are more comfortable and less spooked. He said it can sometimes make a big difference, particularly in the shallow waters of the Cunnigar at low tide.

I arrived at Arthur's house a couple of hours before low tide, after several wrong turns (I must get myself a Sat Nav!) Arthur invited me in for a cuppa and a chat and showed me his fishing diaries that he has kept over the years. I was in shock. I couldn't believe my eyes. Some days he had managed to catch over 50 Bass!! He admitted that on trips where the Bass are so plentiful, he actually packed up and went home as he found no challenge in it whatsoever. I certainly wouldn't mind experiencing that at least once myself!

The Oysters beds.

Arthur's diaries were precise and detailed. He recorded the amount of fish he had caught each day, their weight, the tide, the bait, the catch on the top hook or bottom hook and many other specifics. He has such an accumulation of data that he has made up his own charts on when the best days of the lunar month are to fish, and his chances of catching a fish on any given day. The solunar tables in this book will also provide anglers with details on the best days to fish each month, but some days may be better than others. If details of catches are kept in a diary, each angler should be able to make their own charts detailing the best of these days to fish in their own area.

We packed up the spinning rods and went down to the Cunnigar just before low tide. A decent pair of chest waders is essential for spinning here as you will do quite a bit of walking. The area is a flat sandy bed and at low tide, you can walk for a couple of miles in water no more than 3 ½ feet deep. There are oyster beds further in, that are home to various species of small fish. I was told that this is one of the reasons why the Bass are here all year round. It is a very enjoyable experience to be able to walk so freely with only sand under your feet and cast your lure in any direction you want. Arthur was using the Bass Bullet, giving it a great darting action in its retrieve. I was using the LC Sammy, a top water lure that gives a 'walk the dog' type action. It is a tremendous lure to use, I would nearly eat it myself it looks so tempting in the water! It is designed to resemble an injured fish flapping on the surface.

'The battle'

After about 20 minutes of walking around waist high in the water, casting in all directions, I notice a swirl at the side of my lure. My heart skipped a beat. You can't take your eyes off a surface lure for even a second. My heart then went into overdrive and flooded my head with blood when out of the water came a Bass, lifting the lure with it. Very often you will see the Bass attack surface lures before they actually take it; I assume trying to kill or slow what they think is an injured fish at the top of the water. But this one wasn't attacking, he was hooked. I could feel every turn of the fish on my rod, the braided line transferring every movement with precision. I fought the fish as he stripped line from my reel several times, and then the feeling that every angler dreads on his rod... nothing. The Bass had thrown the hook and won the battle. You have to love them!

We continued spinning and after another half an hour, Arthur had one hooked. He had mentioned to me on the retrieve just before, that he has seen a Bass chasing the lure, but moved off. The fish must have had second thoughts about passing up the meal the first time. It looked like a fabulous fight between the Bass and Arthur. Even after we thought the fish had tired and was just about to be plucked out of the water, he swam for all he was worth, stripping line from Arthur's reel like there was no tomorrow. This happened several times. Truly a fantastic fish! Arthur finally lifted the fine 5lb Bass out of the water and after a quick click of my camera, he

This 5lb Bass couldn't resist the bass bullet.

was returned to fight another day. We walked around for another hour or so, and decided to head back to Arthur's for a cuppa and bit of apple tart before setting out again to do a spot of fishing from the beach.

After a few slices of tart and several cups of tea, we drove back to the Cunni-gar and along the bank to the right, a spit leading in towards Dungarvan town. We set up shop beside some rocks and cast out 30-40 yards. Both of us were using very light rods as there was no need for 6-7oz weights down here. We both used 3 hook flapper traces with size 2/0 hooks and 2-3oz weights. Lug-worm was choice bait, freshly dug by Arthur in the morning.

We decided we wouldn't stay long as I had a friend over on holidays at home that I had to meet, so two hours was the limit. Arthur didn't need very long to get going though. After about 20 minutes his rod buckled over in the stand. What a bite, the rod pounded up and down like a drummers arm. This fish also put up a great fight and after a struggle, was reeled up onto the beach. He was a decent sized fella, about 3 to 3 ½ lbs.

Arthur at what he does best.

After an hour of non-stop bites I still did not have a fish. Arthur was pretty sure by the bites that they were probably the prized Gilthead Bream that the area has become known for. It just wasn't my day, but I wasn't worried, I was well used to it! Arthur uses a great technique to ensure he hooks his fish. He re-uses the lug from previous casts, and slides it up further along the hooklength just above the fresh bait each time. Therefore, when he gets a bite, he wouldn't be certain if the fish was biting around the hook or further up the line. To ensure the fish does feed around the hook, Arthur pulls the line in a foot or two, leaving the fish behind the bait. Then, when the fish bites again, he is fairly sure he has moved up and is feeding at bait on the hook.

This system proved to be successful as he hooked into a lovely fish, putting up an enormous fight. It took Arthur a while to land the fish, and low and behold, it was a fine 3 ½ lb Mullet. I have never seen Mullet being caught on Lugworm, but then again, I see something new every single time I go fishing.

A hard fighting mullet is reeled in.

The whole day was extremely enjoyable and I look forward to the day I can get down to the Cunnigar again for a day's fishing with Arthur. He has an endless amount of stories, be they about fishing or his colourful life, it was a pleasure to fish with him. Arthur is well known throughout Irish angling circles, and has featured in several magazine articles. People come from all parts of Europe for Arthur's excellent Guide service, and I doubt he ever disappoints. I asked Arthur if he was famous in Dungarvan for his fishing success. His response was: 'Famous, not really. Notorious, definitely'.

Contact information:

Arthur Daly - Guide:

Tel: 058-45184

Arthur can also be contacted on sea-angling-ireland.org under the username: Cortaz

SKATE FISHING IN COURTMACSHERRY, CO. CORK

Courtmacsherry is a beautiful little fishing village situated about 30 miles west of Cork City, and has established itself as one of Ireland's premier angling locations. The clean Atlantic waters warmed by the Gulf Stream add to the prolific marine life and species of fish which live off the shore. Year after year, anglers in Courtmacsherry continue to catch the largest quantity of specimen fish in Ireland. In 2007, over 80 specimen fish were landed, which included Cod, Pollack, Conger, Coalfish, Dogfish, Dab and several Bass.

Courtmacsherry angling Ltd is situated on the pier in Courtmacsherry. The purpose built angling boats, the Lady Patricia and the Lady Louise were designed with the angler's comfort and safety in mind. The cruising speed of 18kts gives the angler more fishing time with shark and wreck fishing just 30 minutes away. Dolphin and Whale watching trips can also be arranged and they also offer clients a fleet of self-drive boats for use in the bay.

It was a windy day when we went down to Cork, a force 5 to 6 easterly wind certainly looked daunting, so much so, 3 other anglers that were to share the charter we were on, decided to pull out at the last minute. All the more room for us we thought! The winds did not stop either of the skippers, Mark and Niall, as they guided both boats through the stormy bay with ease. Three skate had been landed on the lady Patricia the day before, the largest being 187lbs so we were eager to get out fishing. First, we had to make a stop off for some fresh bait, Mackerel being the choice fish. After 20 minutes, the box was half full, plenty for 5 Skate anglers, so off we went to known Skate grounds, about 6 miles south of Courtmacsherry.

Once we reached the Skate grounds, we anchored up. This was no easy feat for the skipper in gale force winds and a strong tidal current. It was only a few days after the full moon springs, so the tides were still very strong and the current was moving at a strong and steady pace.

First to catch a fish was Hans, a Dutch angler. He pulled up a decent 15lb conger. After this, several more congers were caught by my fisherman friends Paul Murphy from Wexford and Bruno Seifert from Switzerland. Paul was unfortunate as, for in the space of about an hour, a skate picked up the bait and was on the line for about 5 minutes but then threw the hook. This happened to Paul no less than 3 times, much to his frustration.

It was coming up to about an hour and a half before the slack tide and the skipper announced we should have a good chance at some Skate fairly soon. No sooner had the words left his mouth when Bruno's reel started clicking. He had a skate on and it was lines up for the rest of us on that side. After about half an hour, another reel started clicking, it was Hans' and he also had

Bruno with his new love.

a skate on. Two Skate being hauled at the same time is a special experience, and very rarely happens. All lines were up and Bruno and Hans' were left to battle it out with their Skate.

Paul hooked into Skate on 3 different occasions but they all managed to escape.

After about 25 minutes of very gently pumping and reeling, Hans landed his Skate, 'a baby' according to Niall the skipper, but still coming in at around 80lbs! The Skate are never weighed; their weight is calculated by measuring the length and wingspan of the fish. This fish was gaffed professionally by the skipper and with the aid of me and Paul, the fish was brought aboard. The fish was tagged, a few pictures taken and released within a couple of minutes. Watching the Skate swim off with a few powerful flaps of its wings is an amazing sight, and for the Skipper, the most amazing part of landing a skate. His passion for skate was amazing, and he didn't stop all day, helping everyone in their quest for the big one.

Skipper Niall O Sullivan (left) with Dutch Angler Hans (right) with his 80lb Skate.

Meanwhile Bruno had been holding onto his Skate for dear life, and with sweat pumping from his face, he reached the hour mark of his battle. The skipper had assisted Bruno for a few minutes earlier and estimated the fish to be a minimum of 150lbs, so I said a silent prayer that I would get to see this fish.

Unfortunately, my prayer was not answered, as after 1 hour and 10 minutes, the Skate managed to throw the hook and the fish was lost. Had there not been 5 other men standing beside him, I'm sure Bruno would have cried! The mood on the boat changed after that, and as we had reached the end of the day, it was time to pack up the gear and head back to Courtmacsherry.

There was a sense of real disappointment at losing the Skate, but we did not forget that the overall fishing was fantastic. Nonstop bites and conger, plenty of Skate taking and dropping the bait and one Skate landed. As we all thanked

Niall for the great fishing and all his help, we had already made up our minds that we were coming back here as soon as possible. I was addicted, as I'm sure will be the case for anyone else who goes Skate fishing down in Courtmacsherry.

Ground, tides and season.

When fishing for Skate, it is best to anchor over suitable mixed ground, and downtide from the stern (dropping your bait and line from the back of the boat). Anchoring will ensure that a scent trail is created and will draw Skate to the baits in the area. The weather conditions don't really come into effect when Skate fishing, however it is preferable to fish in milder conditions, as a strong wind will create a large swell that may move your bait up and down off the bottom as the boat moves over the swell. As stated earlier, if the tides are running too fast, it may hinder your chances at catching a Skate so a tide closer to the neaps (first or last quarter moon) and fishing in and around the slack tide (turn of tide) will prove most successful. Skate are caught all year round; however, summer and early autumn prove most successful.

Rod, reel and tackle.

Due to the sheer weight, size and pulling power of the skate, it is important that every skate angler be properly equipped. A rod of 40-50lb class would be suitable and one with roller guides will reduce friction on the line, reducing the chances of losing a fish! As for reels, a good strong boat multiplier is necessary, loaded with 40-50lb line. The line choice is up to the angler, however, when fishing for Skate in depths of 50 meters or so, it would be beneficial to use braid for 2 main reasons:
1. Bite detection is much better.
2. As the braid is smaller in diameter, the line doesn't get caught in the current as much.
All gear should be in good shape, reels and rods well oiled, any frayed line removed from the reel etc. Don't forget, if you hook into a 180lb Skate, it is similar to reeling in a 13 stone person. It would be easier to haul in a person, as they would not have the massive wingspan or pulling power of a Skate so make sure your tackle is ship shape!

The boom rig shown below is the simplest and most successful bottom fishing rig for Skate as shown to us by skipper Niall. A running boom is needed to attach a weight (minimum of 1lb) which should be slid onto the main line. Under this comes a 150lb swivel and then 100 lb hook length mono line about 3 to 4 feet long and finally a size 8/0 to 10/0 hook. The hook should be curved sideways at the barb and hook point to ensure better hooking of the skate.

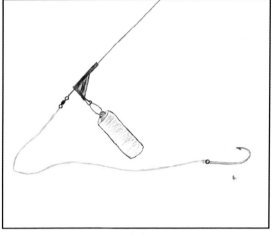

Bottom Fishing Rig.

Bait

Although several baits can be used, Mackerel is the most successful. At first, a Mackerel flapper, as shown on the next page, can be used to create an excellent scent trail; however, for more precise hooking of the Skate, a double fillet can be used on the hook.

The bite

A Skate bite can be identified by a series of short slow nods, where the Skate is settling over the bait. The Skate will then take in the hook and bait and slowly move away, which can be identified by a slow, strong drag on the reel. Allow the Skate to move a little at first and slowly setting the hook by taking the weight on the rod. Reeling in the Skate can be very difficult; however, it is imperative that the drag is set to allow the Skate to run. Through a very gentle pumping action, reel in the fish. But you must keep a constant tension on the line. The more jerking of the line, the bigger the hole gets where the hook is set. This increases the risk of the Skate throwing the hook. Once aboard, please ensure all photographs are taken quickly, so the Skate can be tagged and released as quickly as possible, allowing it to fight another day!

Contact information:

Courtmacsherry Angling Ltd., Woodpoint House, Courtmacsherry, West Cork, Ireland

Mob +353 86 8250905

T: +353 23 464 27

www.courtmacsherryangling.ie   **email: csal@iol.ie**

Mackerel Flapper

Start at the tail end - ensure you use a sharp knife.

Run the knife towards the head along the backbone.

Do the same on the other side, and cut through the backbone.

Remove the tail and back bone piece.

You are then left with the head, guts and flapping fillets.

Run hook into the mouth and through the top of the head.

SPECIMEN FISH

A specimen is a fish which has reached a defined size or weight. The size given to specimens each year is based on the likelihood of catching a fish of that size, factoring in the current distribution of the species and their maximum achievable weight.

To have a specimen fish or a new record ratified, published and/or recorded you need to register a claim with the ISFC. The ISFC listings of record and specimen fish are the official record and are regularly quoted nationally and internationally and the Committee is exhaustive in ensuring that standards are maintained. Adherence to the rules is important to ensure the claim is ratified.

Irish Specimen Fish Committee

The ISFC was established in 1955 and is well regarded by anglers. This Committee consists of representatives of the Irish Angling Federations, Government Departments and official organisations interested in angling. Its objective is to verify, record and publicise the capture of large fish (marine and freshwater) on rod and line in Irish waters. The Committee also ratifies Irish record rod-caught fish. A list is published annually by the Committee.

The Committee is currently examining the issue of "Conservation Specimens" and will continue over the next two years. Two species, Tope and Blue Shark, will be considered for this type of alternative specimen award. It is planned to examine the feasibility of using length measurements to establish a conservation specimen which will allow anglers to return fish to the water quickly without the current requirement to weigh on land.

Many aspects of this proposed system including certification of measuring instruments, the types of measurement(s) required, threshold lengths etc., remain to be discussed and the Committee would welcome written inputs from anglers and all interested parties. Information on all ISFC activities, downloadable claim forms etc., is available on its website www.irish-trophy-fish.com

2007 Records

2007 produced four diverse new Irish records. Records have been established for Gilthead Bream, Garfish, Albacore and Red Mullet. The Committee, having received numerous claims in accordance with ISFC protocol, has added the Blackmouth dogfish (Galeus melastomus) to the specimen list

GILTHEAD BREAM – *Robert McClean from Dublin with his new record of 3.24 kg from Cork Harbour on 10th September 2007.*

RED MULLET – *Joe Cooney from Achill with his new record of 0.71 kg taken at Achill Island on 30th August 2007.*

ALBACORE – *Henry McAuley from Kerry (left) with his new record of 29.96 kg taken on 5th Sep. 2007 in Caherciveen.*

GARFISH – *Stephen O'Neill from Cork with his new record of 1.729 kg taken in Cork Harbour on 28th May 2007.*

Overview of ISFC Rules for Specimen Fish Claimants

Fair Angling: "Fair Angling" means any legitimate method of angling with rod and reel which is recognised as a fair and sporting method. A fish must be hooked in or in the immediate vicinity of the mouth when it has taken the bait or lure; fish which have been foul-hooked, even accidentally, are not eligible. A fish in respect of which a claim is made must be hooked, played and brought to gaff or net by the angler unaided, though the fish may be gaffed or netted by another, and it is permissible for the person using the gaff to take hold of the trace or doubled line (in the case of big game fishing) to steady the fish when it has been played out and brought within reach. If a fixed rod holder is in use while boat fishing, and a fish strikes, the rod must be removed from the holder as quickly as possible. This is to ensure that the angler hooks and plays the fish with rod in hand. Where a fighting chair is employed, it must not have any mechanically driven device which aids the angler in playing a fish. Body harnesses (which attach the rod to the body) are permissible but must not be fixed to the chair. Gimbals must be free swinging including those which move in the vertical plane. Gimbals which permit the angler to rest or reduce strain while playing a fish are prohibited. Breakage of rod, reel or line, or alteration or substitution of tackle, while a fish is being played, disqualify it for claim or record purposes. A fish may not be shot, lanced, clubbed or harpooned before landing. Claims for fish caught during the statutory close season for the species (where this applies) cannot be accepted.

Weighing: Fish must be weighed in the presence of independent, reliable witnesses on certified scales, e.g., a shop scales or an official club scales which is covered by a certificate from the Weights and Measures Officer. All club and personal scales must be certified annually by an independent agency (e.g. Legal Metrology Service). Weighing scales must be covered by a Certificate of Accuracy at the time of weighing and cannot be certified in retrospect, i.e. after the fish has been weighed. Claims cannot be accepted in respect of fish weighed on scales inappropriate to the size of the fish, e.g., fish in the 1 to 3 kg range weighed on balances weighing up to 50 kg or over and graduated in large divisions. Where weights are in large divisions (e.g. 1 lb/1 kg divisions) the weight of a fish must be rounded down to the nearest division. Claims cannot be accepted in the case of fish which have been weighed on board a boat.

Identification: The identification of a fish must be fully documented where there is a possibility of its confusion with any other (and particularly larger) species. For this reason, the Committee, in respect of some species, insists that scales from the fish, close up photographs or the actual body must be forwarded as actual proof of identification, before it will consider claims. Fish scales must be submitted in respect of claims for: Salmon, Sea Trout, Brown Trout (Including Slob Trout). Any brown trout taken in tidal waters, i.e., in the sea or in an estuary below the freshwater boundary as defined for that river will be regarded for claim purposes as a slob trout. About 50 scales scraped from each shoulder of the fish should be sent with the claim.

Fish scales and clear, sharp, close-up photographs must be submitted in respect of claims for: Dace, Rudd, Rudd/Bream Hybrid, Roach, Roach/Bream Hybrid. The ISFC requests that anglers who catch specimens of these species or hybrids would take a small sample of scales (5 to 10 scales) from the fish and place them in a dry envelope (not in a plastic bag or tin foil). This sample, together with good quality colour photographs showing the entire fish on its side and fins well displayed, the dorsal and the anal fins (fully splayed), with additional close up photographs of the head (side on) should be forwarded with each claim form for identification. The scales will be used to positively identify these fish by genetic fingerprinting. This process began in 2007 and, combined with good quality photographic evidence, has provided positive identifications. It also presents the possibility of correctly identifying Rudd/roach hybrids and anglers are invited to submit claims for possible specimens (> 1 kg) of this hybrid in 2008.

The actual body must be forwarded for identification in the case of the following species: Mackerel, Scad, Herring, Shad, Flounder, Dab, Brill, Megrim, Grey & Red Gurnards, Grey Mullet, Golden Grey and Red Mullet, Angler Fish, Lesser Spotted Dogfish, Three Bearded Rockling, Smooth Hound, Rays Bream, Cuckoo Wrasse, Torsk, 'River Eels' taken in tidal waters and Garfish (head and gills only). Claims may be ratified where a photograph is of sufficient quality to provide conclusive evidence (i.e. key identification features clearly visible) to identify a fish, to the satisfaction of the Committee. However, the onus to provide suitable evidence rests solely with the angler.

Clear, sharp, close-up photographs, showing the entire fish with its fins and other features easily seen, and not fore-shortened or obscured by shadows or bystanders must be provided in the case of: Tope, Sharks, Skate, Rays, Bluemouth, Monkfish, Pollock, Coalfish, Ballan Wrasse, Trigger Fish, Albacore, Tub Gurnard (pectoral fins of gurnard must be fully expanded), Gilthead Bream (whole body and head shot showing mouth and eyes).

In the case of skates and rays, photographs of both back and belly surfaces should be provided and particulars of the coloration given (with particular reference to the presence of dark or grey spots, or streaks or patches on the belly side). Samples of the teeth should be furnished in the case of Porbeagle and Mako Sharks. In addition, there should be a clear close-up photograph showing the jaws and teeth exposed.

AWARDS: Anglers whose claims have been accepted by the Committee will be awarded a certificate, a special "Merit Badge" and details of their catch will be published in the full colour annual report. Special awards including a Silver Medal for Record Fish, and different medals for multiple captures accumulated over the years are awarded annually. Only one merit badge will be awarded to any angler per annum even where multiple claims are received.

Limitation on number of claims: A maximum of three (3) awards will be made to any particular claimant for a single species in any one year. However, provision will be made that when an angler achieves this target and subsequently captures larger fish, these will be taken into account but the final number of awards for any species in a single year will not be more than three awards. By including this latter provision, it will ensure that the angler's competitive spirit is kept up and higher achievements could still be sought.

Sending Fish to the Committee

(1) Notify the Committee when a fish is being sent in for identification Telephone 01-884 2600; Fax: 01-836 0060. E-mail: info@cfb.ie
(2) Do not forward fish to the Committee before Bank Holidays or weekends; (keep in a cold store or preferably frozen if fish cannot be delivered quickly

on or before Friday afternoon).

(3) Please attach a label to each fish forwarded for identification giving the captor's name and address, date and place of capture and the weight of the fish.

(4) Fish should not be sent in polythene bags or wrapped in aluminium foil as this causes very rapid decomposition. They should be wrapped in greaseproof paper and then in newspaper and brown paper.

Completed claim forms should be sent to:
The Irish Specimen Fish Committee, Swords Business Campus, Balheary Road, Swords, Co. Dublin, Rep. of Ireland (Tel. 00-353-1-884 2600) before 30th November each year. Where required for identification purposes (see Rule 4) fish should be sent to the same address.

Claims for freshwater fish taken in Northern Ireland can be sent to the ISFC in Dublin or to Dr Robert Rosell, AFBINI, Newforge Lane, BELFAST BT9 5PX. Tel: +44 (0) 28-90255236; Fax: 028-90255004; e-mail: robert.rosell@af-bini.gov.uk

Claims for marine fish taken in Northern Ireland can be sent to the ISFC in Dublin or to Dr Richard Briggs, AFBINI, Newforge Lane, BELFAST BT9 5PX. Tel: +44 (0) 28 90255503; Email: richard.briggs@afbini.gov.uk

Information

The tables over the next 2 pages indicate the current Irish records and specimen weights. These are correct at the time of printing, September 2008; however, record and specimen weights are reviewed annually. Some weights quoted at 3 decimal places were rounded up to 2 decimal places to facilitate layout restrictions in this book. Therefore, please check up to date specimen and records weights in 2009 if in any doubt.

For this information and any further information, as well as download of claim forms and details of record and specimen freshwater fish, please visit www.irish-trophy-fish.com.

Species	Record Weight	Place of Capture	Captor	Specimen Weight
Angler Fish	42.985 kg	Belfast Lough	Sean Neill	18.14 kg (40 lbs)
Bass	17 lbs 13 oz	Doughmore	Emmet Naughton	4.536 kg (10 lbs)
Black Sole	6.32 lbs	Ballycotton	Eddie Cull	0.907 kg (2 lbs)
Bluemouth	2.4 lbs	Caherciveen	Hugh Maguire	0.9 kg (1.99 lbs)
Brill	9 lbs 8 oz	Causeway Coast	Deborah Gregg	2.268 kg (5lbs)
Coalfish	15.1 kg	Castletownshend	Roger Barham	6.804kg (15lbs)
Cod	42 lbs	Ballycotton	I.L. Stewart	9.072kg (20lbs)
Conger Eel	72 lbs	Valentia	J. Green	18.144kg (40lbs)
Dab	2 lbs 5.5 oz	Cork Harbour	Mick Duff	0.680kg (1.5lbs)
Spur Dogfish	21.25 lbs	Dun Laoghaire	Charlie Robinson	5.443kg (12lbs)
Greater Spotted Dogfish	23 lbs 13 oz	Kenmare Bay	Perry Dumay	7.257kg (16lbs)
Lesser Spotted Dogfish	4 lbs 4 oz	Valentia	Cor Heinis	1.48kg (3.25lbs)
Dogfish - Blackmouthed	-	-	-	1 kg (2.21 lbs)
Flounder	4.91 lbs	Ballyteigue	Brian Russell	1.1 kg (2.43 lbs)
Garfish (B. bellone)	1.729 kg	Cork Harbour	Stephen O'Neill	1.02kg (2.25lbs)
Garfish (B. svetovidovi)	1.11 lbs	Courtmacsherry	Eric Leijten	0.36kg (0.88lbs)
Gilthead Bream	3.24 Kg	Cork Harbour	Robert McClean	1.4 kg (3.08lbs)
Tub Gurnard	12 lbs 3.5 oz	Bullsmouth	Robert Seaman	2.268kg (5lbs)
Grey Gurnard	3 lbs 1 oz	Rosslare Bay	Brendan Walsh	0.680kg (1.5lbs)
Red Gurnard	3 lbs 9.5 oz	Belmullet	James Prescott	0.907kg (2lbs)
Haddock	10 lbs 13.5	Kinsale	F.A.E. Bull	3.175kg (7lbs)
Hake	25 lbs 5.5 oz	Belfast Lough	H. W. Steele	4.536kg (10lbs)
Halibut	156 lbs	Belmullet	Frank Brogan	22.680kg (50lbs)
Herring	0.425 kg	Rathlin Island	Wm. McMath	0.34kg (0.75lbs)
John Dory	7 lbs 8 oz	Killala Bay	Cleona Walkin	1.814kg (4lbs)
Ling	55 lbs	Cork Harbour	Ailbhe O'Sullivan	11.34kg (25lbs)
Mackerel	4 lbs 2 oz	Ballycotton	Ulrich Plassmann	1.134kg 2.5lbs
Megrim	1.85 kg	Killala	Paul Hennigan	0.79kg (1.75lbs)
Monkfish	73 lbs	Fenit, Co. Kerry	James Boyd	Suspended
Grey (thick lipped) Mullet	9.10 lbs	Cork Harbour	Cay Heerwagen	2.268kg (5lbs)
Golden Grey Mullet	1.191kg	Cork Harbour	Noel Lane	0.68 kg (1.5lbs)
Red Mullet	0.71 kg	Achill	Joe Cooney	0.454kg (1lb)
Plaice	8.23 lbs	Ballycotton Pier	Edmund Cull	1.814kg (4lbs)
Pollack	19 lbs 3 oz	Ballycotton	J.N. Hearne	5.443kg (12lbs)
Pouting	4 lbs 13.5 oz	Kilmore Quay	John Devereaux	1.361kg (3lbs)

Species	Record Weight	Place of Capture	Captor	Specimen Weight
Thornback Ray	37 lbs	Ling Rocks	M. J. Fitzgerald	9.072kg (20lbs)
Blonde Ray	37 lbs	Cobh	Paul Tennant	11.340kg (25lbs)
Sting Ray	33.2 kg	Tralee Bay	Michael Wall	13.608kg (30lbs)
Cuckoo Ray	5 lbs 11 0z	Causeway Coast	V Morrison	2.041kg (4.5lbs)
Undulate Ray	18 lbs	Fenit	Ann-Mari Liedecke	Suspended
Homelyn Ray	8.28 lbs	Cork Harbour	Edmund Cull	2.268kg(5lbs)
Painted Ray	17.21 lbs	Garryvoe	Edmund Cull	4.536kg (10lbs)
Electric Ray	40 kg	Achill	Shay Boylan	9.072 kg (20lbs)
Ray's Bream	6 lbs 4.25 oz	Valentia	Martin Sarney	2.268kg (5lbs)
Red Sea Bream	9 lbs 6 oz	Valentia	P. Maguire	2.041kg (4.5lbs)
Scad	1.97 lbs	Clonakilty	Mr R. McCarthy	0.680kg (1.5lbs)
Twaite Shad	1.54 kg	St. Mullins	Michael O'Leary	1.1kg (2.4255lbs)
Allis Shad	-	-	-	1.814 kg (4lbs)
Porbeagle Shark	365 lbs	Keem Bay	Dr. O'Donel Brown	68.1kg (150lbs)
Blue Shark	206 lbs	Achill Head	J. McMonagle	45.36kg (100lbs)
Six Gilled Shark	154 lbs	Kinsale	Andrew Bull	45.36kg (100lbs)
Mako Shark	-	-	-	90.72 kg (200lbs)
Thresher Shark	-	-	-	54.43 kg (120lbs)
Common Skate	221 lbs	Ballycotton	T. Tucker	Suspended
White Skate	165 lbs	Clew Bay	Jack Stack	54.43kg (120lbs)
Long Nosed Skate	-	-	-	36.287 kg (80lbs)
Smooth Hound	16.58 lbs	Carne	Keith Gray	3.175kg (7lbs)
Stone Basse	11.72 lbs	Baltimore	Tony Rainer	3.628kg (8lbs)
Three Bearded Rockling	3 lbs 1 oz	Arklow	Maurice Laurent	0.794kg (1.75lbs)
Tope	66 lbs 8 oz	Carlingford L.	Cyril Young	18.144kg (40lbs)
Torsk	4.858 kg	Downings	Jan de Bakker	2.721kg (6lbs)
Trigger Fish	2.54 kg	Slea Head	Bob Moss	1.474kg (3.25lbs)
Turbot	34 lbs	Cork Harbour	Frank Fleming	8.165kg (18lbs)
Tuna - Albacore	29.96 kg	Caherciveen	Henry McAuley	12kg (26.46lbs)
Tuna - Bluefin	440 kg	Donegal Bay	Adrian Molloy	250kg (551.9 lbs)
Whiting	4 lbs 14.5 oz	Kenmare Bay	Cdt.M.J. O'Connor	1.361kg (3lbs)
Ballan Wrasse	4.3 kg	Clogher Head	Bertrand Kron	2.154kg (4.75lbs)
Cuckoo Wrasse	2 lbs 7 oz	Causeway Coast	Brian McLoughlin	0.567kg (1.25lbs)
Salmon	57 lbs	River Suir	M. Maher	9.072 kg (20lbs)
Sea Trout	16 lbs 6 oz	Shimna River	Thomas McManus	2.722 kg (6lbs)

Tide Tables

Tides are caused by the gravitational pull of the moon and the sun on the earth's surface. As the moon is closer than the sun, its pull is around twice the strength of the sun's which is why the tides are mainly influenced by the position of the moon. The tidal effect on the earth's waters is caused by the pull of the moon on the water, creating a bulge that follows it in its rotation of the earth. A bulge is also formed on the opposite side of the planet, as the earth is pulled by the moon a bulge of water is left behind it.

Spring Tides:
When the sun, moon and earth are aligned, the forces of the sun and moon are combined, creating a larger bulge or tide as we know it. There are two instances of this. When the sun and the moon are at opposite sides of the earth, both of their gravitational pulls are exerted on the earth's water creating large tides. This is a full moon tide, i.e., you will see the full moon at nighttime because the sun is at the opposite side of the earth shining light on it. The other instance is when both the sun and the moon are in alignment on the same side of the earth and their gravitational forces are combined. This creates an even larger tide which is called a new moon tide. You will not see the moon in the sky as the sun is behind it, casting its light on the far side.

Neap tides:
Neap tides occur when the sun and the moon are at 90 degrees to each other and slightly cancel out each other's gravitational pull. This creates much smaller tides which are at their smallest during the first and last quarter moon.

Every angler should be aware of the times of low and high tide before going fishing as the tides can leave you stranded on rocks or sandbanks very quickly.

The tide tables over the next few pages are the times of high and low water (tide) and height of water in metres for Dublin Port for the 2009 year. The list of secondary ports on the opposite page shows the difference in times and height for each port from Dublin Port. Variants are also quoted for spring tides and neap tides. **Some of the time differences calculated for secondary ports are average time variants and the tables should NOT be used for navigational purposes.**

Time Variants for Secondary Ports

Secondary Port	Springs Time	HM	Neaps Time	HM	Secondary Port	Springs Time	HM	Neaps Time	HM
Dublin (North Wall)	00 00	0.0	00 00	0.0	Inishgort	-05 42	-0.1	-05 26	+0.2
Dun Laoghaire	-00 06	0.0	-00 01	0.0	Inishbiggle	-05 22	-0.7	-05 12	-0.2
Greystones	-00 08	-0.5	-00 08	-0.5	Broadhaven	-05 37	-0.8	-05 22	-0.4
Wicklow	-00 19	-1.5	-00 19	-1.0	Killala Bay	-05 42	-0.7	-05 17	-0.5
Arklow	-03 15	-2.5	-02 01	-2.0	Ballysadare Bay	-05 18	-0.6	-05 01	-0.2
Courtown	-03 28	-3.0	-02 42	-2.5	Sligo Harbour	-05 34	-0.4	-05 16	-0.2
Wexford Harbour	-04 38	-2.2	-04 45	-1.9	Mullaghmore	-05 41	-0.8	-05 24	-0.3
Rosslare	-05 15	-2.3	-05 39	-2.0	Donegal Harbour	-05 39	-0.6	-05 21	-0.2
Kilmore Quay	-05 43	-0.4	-06 02	-0.6	Killybegs	-05 37	-0.4	05 22	-0.2
Fethard On Sea	-05 58	-0.1	-06.07	-0.2	Loughros More	-05 35	-0.5	-05 17	-0.2
Dunmore East	-05 54	0.0	-06 08	-0.2	Burtonport	-05 35	-0.6	-05 16	-0.3
Dungarvan Harbour	-05 58	-0.1	-05 59	-0.1	Inishboffin Bay	-05 37	-0.6	-05 40	-0.2
Youghal	-06 02	-0.3	-06 01	-0.3	Downies Bay	-05 20	-0.5	-05 29	-0.2
Ballycotton	-06 13	-0.1	-06 12	-0.2	Fanad Head	-05 02	-0.5	-05 31	-0.2
Cobh	-06 02	-0.1	-06 11	-0.2	Rathmullan	-04 52	-0.2	-05 21	0.0
Roberts Cove	-06 07	-0.2	-06 16	-0.2	Trawbreaga Bay	-05 02	-0.5	-05 12	-0.1
Kinsale	-06 21	-0.3	-06 16	-0.2	Culdaff Bay	-04 57	-1.3	-05 08	-1.2
Courtmacsherry	-06 27	-0.2	-06 19	-0.3	River Foyle	-03 54	-1.5	-03 47	-1.6
Clonakilty Bay	-06 35	-0.4	-06 22	-0.4	Warren L.H.	-04 49	-1.8	-05 02	-1.6
Castletownshend	-06 22	-0.5	-06 41	-0.4	Quigleys Point	-04 14	-1.8	-04 14	-1.7
Baltimore	-06 27	-0.7	-06 16	-0.5	Portrush	-04 33	-2.2	-04 28	-2.1
Dunmanus harbour	-07 09	-0.8	-06 42	-0.8	Ballycastle Bay	-02 28	-2.8	-04 59	-2.5
Bantry	-06 47	-0.8	-06 36	-0.8	Cushendun	-00 16	-2.2	-01 02	-2.0
Castletown BH.	-06 50	-1.0	-06 23	-0.8	Red Bay	-00 04	-2.4	-00 42	-2.0
Dunkerron harbour	-07 19	-0.3	-06 38	-0.5	Larne	-00 35	-1.0	-00 42	-1.0
West Cove	-07 15	-0.7	-07 00	-0.7	Carrickfergus	-00 21	-0.8	-00 27	-0.8
Knightstown	-07 20	-0.7	-06 49	-0.6	Belfast	-00 26	-0.5	-00 32	-0.5
Cromane Point	-06 28	+0.3	-06 17	0.0	Donaghadee	-00 06	0.0	-00 12	-0.1
Dingle Harbour	-07 13	-0.2	-06 52	-0.2	Killard Point	-00 15	+0.5	-00 11	+0.3
Smerwick Harbour	-07 09	-0.4	-06 38	-0.6	Killough Harbour	-00 26	+1.3	-00 12	+1.1
Fenit Pier	-06 59	+0.4	-06 28	0.0	Newcastle	-00 01	+1.1	+00 03	+0.6
Tarbet Island	-05 51	+0.7	-05 44	+0.7	Kilkeel	+00 14	+0.7	-00 02	+0.6
Kilbaha Bay	-06 36	0.0	-06 09	+0.2	Warrenpoint	-00 20	+1.0	-00 10	+0.7
Liscannor	-06 20	+0.2	-06 19	+0.4	Soldiers Point	-00 10	+1.0	-00 10	+0.8
Galway	-06 17	+0.6	-06 12	+0.7	Dunany Point	-00 28	+0.7	-00 18	+0.9
Kilkieran Cove	-06 12	+0.3	-06 07	+0.5	River Boyne Bar	-00 05	+0.4	00 00	+0.3
Roundstone Bay	-06 14	-0.1	-06 09	+0.2	Balbriggan	-00 21	+0.3	-00 15	+0.2
Clifden Bay	-06 12	-0.1	-06 07	+0.2	Malahide	+00 02	+0.1	+00 03	-0.2
Kilary Harbour	-05 56	-0.4	-05 57	-0.1	Howth	-00 07	0.0	-00 05	-0.1

Tide Tables

JANUARY 2009   DUBLIN (NORTH WALL)

HEIGHTS ABOVE CHART DATUM

		High Water				Low Water			
Date		Morning		Afternoon		Morning		Afternoon	
		Time	m	Time	m	Time	m	Time	m
1	TH	02 13	3.6	14 25	3.9	07 42	1.2	20 13	0.9
2	F	02 56	3.6	15 08	3.9	08 25	1.2	20 56	1.0
3	SA	03 42	3.5	15 54	3.8	09 12	1.3	21 43	1.0
4	SU ☽	04 33	3.5	16 45	3.7	10 04	1.4	22 37	1.1
5	M	05 30	3.4	17 42	3.6	11 04	1.4	23 38	1.2
6	TU	06 34	3.4	18 47	3.6			12 12	1.4
7	W	07 41	3.5	19 59	3.6	00 49	1.2	13 24	1.4
8	TH	08 44	3.7	21 07	3.8	01 59	1.2	14 30	1.2
9	F	09 41	3.9	22 08	3.9	03 01	1.1	15 30	0.9
10	SA	10 33	4.1	23 02	4.0	03 55	0.9	16 24	0.6
11	SU ○	11 21	4.3	23 52	4.1	04 43	0.8	17 13	0.4
12	M			12 07	4.4	05 27	0.7	18 00	0.3
13	TU	00 39	4.1	12 54	4.4	06 10	0.7	18 46	0.3
14	W	01 27	4.0	13 41	4.3	06 54	0.7	19 34	0.4
15	TH	02 15	3.9	14 30	4.2	07 40	0.8	20 23	0.5
16	F	03 04	3.7	15 20	4.1	08 30	1.0	21 13	0.7
17	SA	03 55	3.6	16 14	3.9	09 24	1.2	22 05	1.0
18	SU ☾	04 51	3.5	17 14	3.6	10 22	1.4	23 01	1.3
19	M	05 53	3.4	18 21	3.5	11 27	1.5		
20	TU	06 58	3.3	19 29	3.4	00 04	1.5	12 42	1.6
21	W	08 01	3.4	20 36	3.3	01 20	1.6	14 07	1.6
22	TH	09 00	3.5	21 37	3.4	02 35	1.6	15 13	1.5
23	F	09 50	3.7	22 25	3.5	03 29	1.5	16 00	1.3
24	SA	10 33	3.8	23 03	3.6	04 09	1.3	16 38	1.1
25	SU	11 09	3.9	23 36	3.6	04 43	1.2	17 09	1.0
26	M ●	11 40	3.9			05 13	1.1	17 38	0.9
27	TU	00 05	3.7	12 10	4.0	05 40	1.0	18 04	0.8
28	W	00 34	3.7	12 41	4.0	06 07	0.9	18 30	0.7
29	TH	01 05	3.8	13 16	4.0	06 37	0.8	19 02	0.7
30	F	01 40	3.8	13 55	4.0	07 12	0.8	19 39	0.7
31	SA	02 20	3.8	14 36	4.0	07 51	0.9	20 20	0.7

Time Zone UT(GMT)

FEBRUARY 2009

DUBLIN (NORTH WALL)

HEIGHTS ABOVE CHART DATUM

		High Water				Low Water			
Date		Morning		Afternoon		Morning		Afternoon	
		Time	m	Time	m	Time	m	Time	m
1	**SU**	03 03	3.7	15 21	3.9	08 35	1.0	21 05	0.9
2	M ☽	03 50	3.6	16 10	3.8	09 25	1.1	21 56	1.0
3	TU	04 45	3.5	17 07	3.6	10 23	1.3	22 56	1.3
4	W	05 52	3.4	18 19	3.5	11 37	1.4		
5	TH	07 12	3.4	19 44	3.5	00 15	1.4	13 03	1.4
6	F	08 27	3.6	21 02	3.6	01 43	1.4	14 22	1.2
7	SA	09 31	3.8	22 05	3.8	02 56	1.2	15 27	0.9
8	**SU**	10 25	4.0	22 57	3.9	03 52	1.0	16 20	0.5
9	M O	11 12	4.2	23 42	4.0	04 36	0.7	17 05	0.3
10	TU	11 55	4.3			05 17	0.6	17 47	0.2
11	W	00 23	4.0	12 36	4.3	05 54	0.5	18 27	0.2
12	TH	01 02	3.9	13 17	4.3	06 33	0.5	19 08	0.3
13	F	01 41	3.9	13 59	4.1	07 14	0.6	19 51	0.5
14	SA	02 21	3.7	14 44	4.0	07 58	0.8	20 34	0.7
15	**SU**	03 04	3.6	15 31	3.7	08 46	1.0	21 21	1.0
16	M ☾	03 52	3.5	16 26	3.5	09 41	1.2	22 12	1.3
17	TU	04 51	3.3	17 34	3.3	10 43	1.4	23 12	1.6
18	W	06 05	3.2	18 52	3.1	11 55	1.6		
19	TH	07 19	3.2	20 06	3.1	00 25	1.7	13 34	1.6
20	F	08 26	3.3	21 13	3.2	02 05	1.7	14 51	1.4
21	SA	09 23	3.5	22 03	3.4	03 08	1.5	15 38	1.2
22	**SU**	10 08	3.7	22 41	3.5	03 48	1.3	16 13	1.0
23	M	10 45	3.8	23 12	3.6	04 20	1.1	16 42	0.9
24	TU	11 15	3.9	23 39	3.7	04 47	0.9	17 08	0.7
25	W ●	11 43	4.0			05 13	0.8	17 32	0.6
26	TH	00 03	3.8	12 13	4.0	05 38	0.7	17 58	0.5
27	F	00 33	3.8	12 47	4.1	06 08	0.6	18 31	0.5
28	SA	01 07	3.9	13 26	4.1	06 43	0.6	19 08	0.5

Time Zone UT(GMT)

MARCH 2009   **DUBLIN (NORTH WALL)**

HEIGHTS ABOVE CHART DATUM

		High Water				Low Water			
Date		Morning		Afternoon		Morning		Afternoon	
		Time	m	Time	m	Time	m	Time	m
1	**SU**	01 47	3.9	14 08	4.0	07 23	0.6	19 49	0.6
2	M	02 30	3.8	14 54	3.9	08 08	0.7	20 36	0.8
3	TU	03 18	3.7	15 46	3.7	09 00	0.9	21 28	1.1
4	W ☽	04 14	3.5	16 47	3.5	10 03	1.1	22 33	1.3
5	TH	05 24	3.4	18 08	3.3	11 24	1.3	23 59	1.5
6	F	06 54	3.3	19 42	3.3			12 55	1.3
7	SA	08 15	3.5	21 00	3.5	01 35	1.5	14 17	1.0
8	**SU**	09 21	3.7	22 00	3.7	02 49	1.2	15 19	0.7
9	M	10 15	4.0	22 49	3.8	03 41	0.9	16 07	0.4
10	TU	11 01	4.1	23 29	3.9	04 23	0.7	16 49	0.3
11	W O	11 41	4.2			05 01	0.5	17 28	0.2
12	TH	00 04	3.9	12 18	4.2	05 37	0.5	18 05	0.2
13	F	00 35	3.9	12 54	4.1	06 12	0.5	18 42	0.4
14	SA	01 08	3.8	13 32	4.0	06 50	0.5	19 19	0.5
15	**SU**	01 44	3.8	14 14	3.8	07 31	0.7	19 59	0.8
16	M	02 24	3.7	14 58	3.6	08 16	0.8	20 43	1.0
17	TU	03 07	3.5	15 49	3.4	09 08	1.1	21 32	1.3
18	W ☾	03 57	3.3	16 53	3.1	10 08	1.3	22 31	1.6
19	TH	05 08	3.2	18 15	3.0	11 18	1.5	23 42	1.7
20	F	06 37	3.1	19 33	3.0			12 42	1.5
21	SA	07 50	3.2	20 40	3.1	01 10	1.7	14 10	1.4
22	**SU**	08 49	3.4	21 31	3.3	02 29	1.5	15 01	1.2
23	M	09 36	3.6	22 09	3.5	03 13	1.3	15 36	1.0
24	TU	10 13	3.7	22 40	3.6	03 46	1.1	16 05	0.8
25	W	10 44	3.8	23 06	3.7	04 14	0.8	16 31	0.6
26	TH ●	11 12	3.9	23 31	3.8	04 41	0.7	16 58	0.5
27	F	11 44	4.0			05 09	0.5	17 28	0.4
28	SA	00 01	3.9	12 21	4.1	05 42	0.4	18 02	0.4
29	**SU**	00 38	4.0	13 02	4.1	06 19	0.4	18 42	0.5
30	M	01 20	3.9	13 48	4.0	07 02	0.5	19 26	0.6
31	TU	02 06	3.9	14 39	3.8	07 52	0.6	20 16	0.9

Time Zone UT(GMT)

APRIL 2009   DUBLIN (NORTH WALL)

HEIGHTS ABOVE CHART DATUM

		High Water				Low Water			
Date		Morning		Afternoon		Morning		Afternoon	
		Time	m	Time	m	Time	m	Time	m
1	W	02 58	3.7	15 36	3.6	08 51	0.8	21 15	1.1
2	TH ☽	03 57	3.6	16 44	3.4	10 01	1.0	22 26	1.4
3	F	05 12	3.4	18 11	3.3	11 22	1.1	23 51	1.5
4	SA	06 42	3.4	19 36	3.4			12 46	1.1
5	**SU**	08 00	3.6	20 48	3.5	01 19	1.4	14 01	0.9
6	M	09 05	3.8	21 45	3.7	02 28	1.2	14 59	0.6
7	TU	10 00	3.9	22 32	3.8	03 20	1.0	15 47	0.5
8	W	10 46	4.0	23 11	3.8	04 03	0.8	16 28	0.4
9	TH ○	11 26	4.1	23 42	3.8	04 42	0.6	17 07	0.4
10	F			12 01	4.0	05 19	0.5	17 42	0.4
11	SA	00 10	3.8	12 35	3.9	05 54	0.5	18 17	0.5
12	**SU**	00 41	3.8	13 11	3.8	06 31	0.6	18 52	0.7
13	M	01 16	3.8	13 51	3.7	07 11	0.7	19 30	0.9
14	TU	01 55	3.7	14 34	3.5	07 55	0.8	20 12	1.1
15	W	02 37	3.6	15 23	3.3	08 45	1.0	21 00	1.3
16	TH	03 24	3.4	16 21	3.1	09 42	1.2	21 58	1.5
17	F ☾	04 24	3.3	17 36	3.0	10 46	1.3	23 06	1.7
18	SA	05 45	3.2	18 51	3.0	11 56	1.4		
19	**SU**	07 03	3.2	19 55	3.1	00 18	1.7	13 07	1.3
20	M	08 04	3.3	20 47	3.3	01 28	1.5	14 04	1.1
21	TU	08 52	3.5	21 28	3.5	02 21	1.3	14 46	0.9
22	W	09 32	3.6	22 01	3.6	03 00	1.1	15 21	0.7
23	TH	10 07	3.8	22 30	3.8	03 34	0.9	15 53	0.6
24	F	10 41	3.9	23 00	3.9	04 07	0.7	16 26	0.5
25	SA ●	11 19	4.0	23 36	4.0	04 41	0.5	17 01	0.4
26	**SU**			12 00	4.1	05 20	0.4	17 40	0.4
27	M	00 16	4.0	12 47	4.0	06 02	0.4	18 23	0.5
28	TU	01 02	4.0	13 38	3.9	06 51	0.4	19 11	0.7
29	W	01 52	3.9	14 33	3.8	07 47	0.6	20 06	0.9
30	TH	02 48	3.8	15 35	3.6	08 50	0.7	21 09	1.2

Time Zone UT(GMT)

MAY 2009 **DUBLIN (NORTH WALL)**

HEIGHTS ABOVE CHART DATUM

Date			High Water				Low Water			
			Morning		Afternoon		Morning		Afternoon	
			Time	m	Time	m	Time	m	Time	m
1	F	☽	03 52	3.7	16 46	3.5	10 00	0.8	22 19	1.3
2	SA		05 06	3.6	18 03	3.4	11 13	0.9	23 34	1.4
3	**SU**		06 25	3.6	19 17	3.4			12 26	0.9
4	M		07 37	3.7	20 23	3.5	00 49	1.4	13 33	0.8
5	TU		08 41	3.8	21 19	3.6	01 56	1.2	14 31	0.7
6	W		09 37	3.9	22 07	3.7	02 52	1.1	15 21	0.6
7	TH		10 26	3.9	22 48	3.7	03 39	0.9	16 05	0.6
8	F		11 08	3.9	23 20	3.8	04 22	0.8	16 45	0.7
9	SA	O	11 44	3.8	23 48	3.8	05 02	0.8	17 21	0.7
10	**SU**				12 18	3.8	05 40	0.7	17 56	0.8
11	M		00 19	3.8	12 54	3.7	06 18	0.8	18 31	0.9
12	TU		00 55	3.8	13 32	3.6	06 57	0.8	19 08	1.0
13	W		01 33	3.8	14 14	3.5	07 39	0.9	19 48	1.1
14	TH		02 15	3.7	14 59	3.4	08 25	1.0	20 33	1.3
15	F		03 00	3.6	15 50	3.3	09 16	1.1	21 25	1.4
16	SA		03 52	3.4	16 49	3.2	10 11	1.2	22 25	1.5
17	**SU**	☾	04 51	3.3	17 54	3.1	11 09	1.3	23 27	1.6
18	M		05 57	3.3	18 58	3.2			12 08	1.2
19	TU		07 01	3.3	19 51	3.3	00 28	1.5	13 03	1.1
20	W		07 56	3.5	20 37	3.4	01 23	1.4	13 52	1.0
21	TH		08 44	3.6	21 17	3.6	02 10	1.2	14 36	0.8
22	F		09 30	3.8	21 55	3.8	02 53	1.0	15 17	0.7
23	SA		10 14	3.9	22 35	3.9	03 35	0.8	15 58	0.6
24	**SU**	●	11 00	4.0	23 17	4.0	04 18	0.6	16 40	0.5
25	M		11 48	4.0			05 04	0.5	17 24	0.6
26	TU		00 02	4.1	12 38	4.0	05 52	0.4	18 10	0.6
27	W		00 51	4.1	13 32	4.0	06 44	0.4	19 01	0.8
28	TH		01 43	4.1	14 29	3.8	07 42	0.5	19 56	0.9
29	F		02 41	4.0	15 29	3.7	08 44	0.6	20 56	1.1
30	SA		03 43	3.9	16 34	3.6	09 48	0.7	22 00	1.2
31	**SU**	☽	04 51	3.9	17 40	3.5	10 52	0.8	23 06	1.3

Time Zone UT(GMT)

JUNE 2009   DUBLIN (NORTH WALL)

HEIGHTS ABOVE CHART DATUM

		High Water				Low Water			
Date		Morning		Afternoon		Morning		Afternoon	
		Time	m	Time	m	Time	m	Time	m
1	M	06 00	3.8	18 47	3.5	11 56	0.8		
2	TU	07 07	3.8	19 49	3.5	00 14	1.3	13 01	0.9
3	W	08 11	3.8	20 47	3.6	01 20	1.3	14 00	0.9
4	TH	09 10	3.8	21 38	3.6	02 22	1.2	14 55	1.0
5	F	10 03	3.7	22 21	3.7	03 17	1.2	15 42	1.0
6	SA	10 49	3.7	22 58	3.7	04 05	1.1	16 24	1.0
7	**SU** O	11 28	3.7	23 30	3.8	04 48	1.0	17 02	1.0
8	M			12 02	3.7	05 28	1.0	17 38	1.0
9	TU	00 01	3.8	12 36	3.6	06 05	0.9	18 11	1.0
10	W	00 36	3.8	13 12	3.6	06 42	0.9	18 46	1.1
11	TH	01 13	3.8	13 51	3.5	07 20	1.0	19 23	1.1
12	F	01 52	3.8	14 31	3.5	07 59	1.0	20 02	1.2
13	SA	02 34	3.7	15 15	3.4	08 41	1.0	20 46	1.3
14	**SU**	03 20	3.7	16 02	3.3	09 25	1.1	21 35	1.3
15	M ☾	04 09	3.6	16 53	3.3	10 14	1.1	22 28	1.4
16	TU	05 02	3.5	17 49	3.3	11 07	1.1	23 25	1.4
17	W	06 00	3.5	18 48	3.3			12 04	1.2
18	TH	07 00	3.5	19 45	3.4	00 25	1.4	13 01	1.1
19	F	08 02	3.6	20 39	3.6	01 23	1.3	13 56	1.0
20	SA	09 01	3.7	21 29	3.8	02 19	1.1	14 49	0.9
21	**SU**	09 56	3.9	22 17	4.0	03 12	0.9	15 39	0.8
22	M ●	10 48	4.0	23 04	4.1	04 03	0.7	16 26	0.7
23	TU	11 39	4.0	23 51	4.2	04 54	0.5	17 13	0.6
24	W			12 29	4.1	05 44	0.4	18 00	0.7
25	TH	00 39	4.3	13 21	4.0	06 35	0.3	18 47	0.7
26	F	01 31	4.3	14 14	3.9	07 29	0.4	19 39	0.8
27	SA	02 25	4.2	15 09	3.8	08 26	0.4	20 33	1.0
28	**SU**	03 22	4.1	16 06	3.7	09 23	0.6	21 31	1.1
29	M ☽	04 23	4.0	17 06	3.6	10 21	0.8	22 31	1.2
30	TU	05 27	3.8	18 08	3.5	11 20	0.9	23 34	1.4

Time Zone UT(GMT)

JULY 2009　　　　　　　　　　　　**DUBLIN (NORTH WALL)**

HEIGHTS ABOVE CHART DATUM

			High Water				Low Water			
Date			Morning		Afternoon		Morning		Afternoon	
			Time	m	Time	m	Time	m	Time	m
1	W		06 34	3.7	19 10	3.5			12 22	1.1
2	TH		07 39	3.6	20 10	3.5	00 43	1.4	13 27	1.2
3	F		08 43	3.6	21 06	3.6	01 54	1.4	14 29	1.3
4	SA		09 41	3.6	21 55	3.7	02 59	1.4	15 22	1.3
5	**SU**		10 31	3.6	22 36	3.7	03 53	1.2	16 07	1.2
6	M		11 11	3.6	23 11	3.8	04 37	1.1	16 45	1.2
7	TU	O	11 45	3.6	23 43	3.9	05 15	1.0	17 19	1.1
8	W				12 17	3.6	05 50	1.0	17 51	1.0
9	TH		00 15	3.9	12 49	3.6	06 21	0.9	18 22	1.0
10	F		00 49	3.9	13 22	3.6	06 52	0.9	18 53	1.0
11	SA		01 25	3.9	13 58	3.6	07 23	0.9	19 28	1.0
12	**SU**		02 04	3.9	14 38	3.6	07 58	0.9	20 07	1.1
13	M		02 46	3.8	15 20	3.5	08 38	0.9	20 50	1.1
14	TU		03 31	3.8	16 06	3.5	09 23	1.0	21 37	1.2
15	W	☾	04 19	3.7	16 58	3.4	10 13	1.1	22 31	1.3
16	TH		05 14	3.6	17 57	3.4	11 10	1.2	23 34	1.4
17	F		06 19	3.5	19 05	3.4			12 16	1.3
18	SA		07 32	3.5	20 12	3.5	00 46	1.4	13 26	1.2
19	**SU**		08 43	3.6	21 12	3.7	01 56	1.2	14 30	1.1
20	M		09 45	3.8	22 05	4.0	02 59	1.0	15 27	1.0
21	TU		10 39	3.9	22 53	4.2	03 56	0.7	16 17	0.8
22	W	●	11 28	4.0	23 39	4.3	04 46	0.4	17 02	0.6
23	TH				12 15	4.1	05 34	0.3	17 46	0.6
24	F		00 24	4.4	13 02	4.0	06 21	0.2	18 29	0.6
25	SA		01 11	4.4	13 49	4.0	07 09	0.3	19 14	0.7
26	**SU**		01 59	4.3	14 37	3.8	07 58	0.4	20 03	0.8
27	M		02 50	4.1	15 27	3.7	08 50	0.6	20 56	1.0
28	TU	☽	03 45	3.9	16 21	3.6	09 43	0.8	21 53	1.2
29	W		04 46	3.7	17 21	3.4	10 38	1.1	22 54	1.4
30	TH		05 55	3.5	18 27	3.4	11 38	1.3		
31	F		07 07	3.4	19 33	3.4	00 04	1.5	12 48	1.5

Time Zone UT(GMT)

AUGUST 2009   DUBLIN (NORTH WALL)

HEIGHTS ABOVE CHART DATUM

			High Water				Low Water			
Date			Morning		Afternoon		Morning		Afternoon	
			Time	m	Time	m	Time	m	Time	m
1	SA		08 18	3.4	20 35	3.5	01 29	1.6	14 03	1.5
2	**SU**		09 23	3.4	21 30	3.6	02 47	1.4	15 04	1.5
3	M		10 14	3.5	22 15	3.8	03 41	1.3	15 49	1.3
4	TU		10 53	3.6	22 51	3.9	04 22	1.1	16 26	1.2
5	W		11 25	3.6	23 23	3.9	04 56	1.0	16 58	1.1
6	TH	O	11 54	3.7	23 52	4.0	05 26	0.9	17 27	1.0
7	F				12 22	3.7	05 53	0.8	17 54	0.9
8	SA		00 21	4.0	12 51	3.7	06 17	0.8	18 22	0.8
9	**SU**		00 55	4.0	13 24	3.7	06 45	0.8	18 54	0.8
10	M		01 32	4.0	14 02	3.7	07 19	0.8	19 31	0.9
11	TU		02 13	4.0	14 43	3.7	07 59	0.8	20 13	1.0
12	W		02 56	3.9	15 28	3.6	08 43	0.9	21 00	1.1
13	TH	☾	03 44	3.7	16 18	3.5	09 32	1.1	21 54	1.2
14	F		04 40	3.6	17 19	3.4	10 31	1.3	23 02	1.4
15	SA		05 49	3.4	18 35	3.4	11 44	1.4		
16	**SU**		07 16	3.4	19 53	3.5	00 25	1.4	13 08	1.4
17	M		08 35	3.5	20 59	3.7	01 47	1.2	14 22	1.3
18	TU		09 38	3.7	21 53	4.0	02 55	0.9	15 20	1.0
19	W		10 30	3.9	22 40	4.2	03 50	0.6	16 07	0.8
20	TH	●	11 16	4.0	23 24	4.4	04 37	0.3	16 49	0.6
21	F		11 58	4.1			05 20	0.2	17 28	0.5
22	SA		00 05	4.4	12 39	4.0	06 01	0.1	18 07	0.5
23	**SU**		00 47	4.4	13 19	4.0	06 43	0.2	18 49	0.6
24	M		01 30	4.3	14 00	3.9	07 27	0.4	19 33	0.7
25	TU		02 16	4.1	14 45	3.7	08 13	0.7	20 22	0.9
26	W		03 06	3.8	15 33	3.6	09 03	1.0	21 17	1.2
27	TH	☽	04 03	3.6	16 30	3.4	09 56	1.3	22 19	1.4
28	F		05 15	3.3	17 41	3.3	10 55	1.5	23 29	1.6
29	SA		06 34	3.2	18 56	3.3			12 05	1.7
30	**SU**		07 52	3.2	20 04	3.4	01 02	1.6	13 33	1.7
31	M		09 02	3.3	21 03	3.6	02 28	1.5	14 41	1.6

Time Zone UT(GMT)

Tide Tables

SEPTEMBER 2009 **DUBLIN (NORTH WALL)**

HEIGHTS ABOVE CHART DATUM

			High Water				Low Water			
Date			Morning		Afternoon		Morning		Afternoon	
			Time	m	Time	m	Time	m	Time	m
1	TU		09 53	3.5	21 50	3.8	03 20	1.2	15 26	1.4
2	W		10 29	3.6	22 27	3.9	03 58	1.1	16 02	1.2
3	TH		11 00	3.7	22 58	4.0	04 29	0.9	16 32	1.0
4	F	O	11 28	3.7	23 25	4.0	04 55	0.8	16 59	0.9
5	SA		11 53	3.8	23 52	4.1	05 19	0.7	17 24	0.8
6	**SU**				12 19	3.8	05 43	0.6	17 52	0.7
7	M		00 24	4.1	12 52	3.9	06 11	0.6	18 24	0.7
8	TU		01 02	4.1	13 29	3.9	06 45	0.7	19 01	0.7
9	W		01 43	4.0	14 11	3.8	07 25	0.8	19 44	0.9
10	TH		02 28	3.9	14 57	3.7	08 10	0.9	20 34	1.0
11	F		03 19	3.7	15 50	3.6	09 03	1.2	21 33	1.2
12	SA	☾	04 19	3.5	16 53	3.4	10 07	1.4	22 49	1.4
13	**SU**		05 37	3.4	18 16	3.4	11 29	1.5		
14	M		07 10	3.4	19 38	3.6	00 18	1.4	12 58	1.5
15	TU		08 29	3.5	20 45	3.8	01 42	1.1	14 12	1.3
16	W		09 30	3.7	21 40	4.0	02 47	0.8	15 08	1.0
17	TH		10 20	3.9	22 27	4.2	03 38	0.5	15 53	0.8
18	F	●	11 02	4.0	23 08	4.3	04 22	0.3	16 33	0.6
19	SA		11 39	4.1	23 46	4.4	05 02	0.2	17 10	0.5
20	**SU**				12 14	4.0	05 40	0.2	17 48	0.5
21	M		00 24	4.3	12 50	4.0	06 18	0.3	18 26	0.6
22	TU		01 05	4.2	13 28	3.9	06 57	0.5	19 09	0.7
23	W		01 48	4.0	14 10	3.8	07 40	0.8	19 56	0.9
24	TH		02 36	3.8	14 55	3.7	08 26	1.1	20 49	1.1
25	F		03 30	3.5	15 48	3.5	09 19	1.4	21 50	1.3
26	SA	☽	04 39	3.3	16 56	3.4	10 19	1.6	22 58	1.5
27	**SU**		06 00	3.1	18 16	3.3	11 28	1.8		
28	M		07 18	3.1	19 28	3.4	00 22	1.6	12 50	1.8
29	TU		08 28	3.3	20 29	3.5	01 52	1.4	14 05	1.6
30	W		09 19	3.5	21 18	3.7	02 45	1.2	14 53	1.4

Time Zone UT(GMT)

88

OCTOBER 2009   **DUBLIN (NORTH WALL)**

HEIGHTS ABOVE CHART DATUM

		High Water				Low Water			
Date		Morning		Afternoon		Morning		Afternoon	
		Time	m	Time	m	Time	m	Time	m
1	TH	09 57	3.6	21 56	3.8	03 24	1.0	15 30	1.2
2	F	10 29	3.7	22 28	3.9	03 54	0.9	16 00	1.0
3	SA	10 57	3.8	22 56	4.0	04 20	0.7	16 28	0.8
4	**SU** ○	11 22	3.9	23 24	4.1	04 44	0.6	16 55	0.7
5	M	11 49	4.0	23 58	4.1	05 11	0.6	17 25	0.7
6	TU			12 22	4.0	05 42	0.6	18 00	0.6
7	W	00 36	4.1	13 02	4.0	06 18	0.7	18 39	0.7
8	TH	01 21	4.0	13 47	3.9	06 59	0.8	19 26	0.8
9	F	02 10	3.9	14 37	3.8	07 48	1.0	20 21	1.0
10	SA	03 06	3.7	15 33	3.7	08 46	1.3	21 27	1.1
11	**SU** ☽	04 12	3.5	16 40	3.6	09 56	1.5	22 45	1.2
12	M	05 35	3.4	18 01	3.6	11 19	1.6		
13	TU	07 01	3.4	19 20	3.7	00 09	1.2	12 42	1.5
14	W	08 14	3.6	20 27	3.9	01 26	1.0	13 51	1.3
15	TH	09 13	3.8	21 23	4.1	02 27	0.8	14 47	1.1
16	F	10 02	3.9	22 11	4.2	03 18	0.6	15 33	0.9
17	SA	10 44	4.0	22 54	4.2	04 02	0.4	16 15	0.7
18	**SU** ●	11 21	4.0	23 32	4.2	04 42	0.4	16 54	0.6
19	M	11 53	4.0			05 20	0.4	17 32	0.6
20	TU	00 08	4.1	12 27	4.0	05 56	0.6	18 11	0.7
21	W	00 47	4.0	13 04	4.0	06 33	0.7	18 52	0.8
22	TH	01 29	3.9	13 44	3.9	07 12	0.9	19 37	0.9
23	F	02 14	3.7	14 28	3.8	07 57	1.2	20 28	1.1
24	SA	03 05	3.5	15 17	3.6	08 47	1.4	21 24	1.3
25	**SU**	04 07	3.3	16 16	3.5	09 46	1.6	22 27	1.4
26	M ☽	05 21	3.2	17 30	3.4	10 52	1.7	23 36	1.5
27	TU	06 35	3.2	18 43	3.4			12 02	1.8
28	W	07 40	3.3	19 44	3.5	00 49	1.5	13 11	1.7
29	TH	08 34	3.4	20 35	3.6	01 52	1.3	14 07	1.5
30	F	09 17	3.6	21 17	3.7	02 37	1.1	14 48	1.3
31	SA	09 52	3.7	21 53	3.9	03 11	1.0	15 23	1.1

Time Zone UT(GMT)

NOVEMBER 2009   DUBLIN (NORTH WALL)

HEIGHTS ABOVE CHART DATUM

		High Water				Low Water			
Date		**Morning**		**Afternoon**		**Morning**		**Afternoon**	
		Time	m	Time	m	Time	m	Time	m
1	**SU**	10 23	3.9	22 25	4.0	03 42	0.8	15 55	0.9
2	M O	10 51	4.0	23 00	4.1	04 11	0.7	16 27	0.8
3	TU	11 23	4.0	23 38	4.1	04 43	0.6	17 03	0.7
4	W			12 00	4.1	05 19	0.6	17 43	0.6
5	TH	00 21	4.1	12 43	4.1	05 58	0.7	18 27	0.7
6	F	01 09	4.0	13 31	4.1	06 43	0.9	19 18	0.7
7	SA	02 02	3.9	14 24	4.0	07 35	1.1	20 17	0.9
8	**SU**	03 02	3.7	15 23	3.9	08 36	1.3	21 23	1.0
9	M ☾	04 09	3.6	16 30	3.8	09 45	1.4	22 34	1.0
10	TU	05 25	3.5	17 43	3.8	11 00	1.5	23 48	1.0
11	W	06 40	3.6	18 55	3.8			12 14	1.5
12	TH	07 48	3.7	20 01	3.9	00 58	1.0	13 22	1.4
13	F	08 47	3.8	21 01	4.0	02 00	0.9	14 21	1.2
14	SA	09 39	3.9	21 54	4.0	02 54	0.8	15 12	1.1
15	**SU**	10 24	4.0	22 40	4.1	03 41	0.7	15 59	1.0
16	M ●	11 03	4.0	23 21	4.0	04 24	0.7	16 41	0.9
17	TU	11 37	4.0	23 57	4.0	05 02	0.8	17 22	0.8
18	W			12 09	4.0	05 39	0.8	18 01	0.8
19	TH	00 34	3.9	12 45	4.0	06 14	0.9	18 41	0.9
20	F	01 13	3.8	13 23	4.0	06 52	1.1	19 23	1.0
21	SA	01 55	3.7	14 05	3.9	07 32	1.2	20 07	1.1
22	**SU**	02 42	3.5	14 50	3.8	08 18	1.3	20 56	1.2
23	M	03 33	3.4	15 39	3.6	09 10	1.5	21 49	1.3
24	TU ☽	04 32	3.3	16 34	3.5	10 09	1.6	22 46	1.4
25	W	05 39	3.2	17 37	3.4	11 12	1.7	23 46	1.4
26	TH	06 43	3.3	18 41	3.4			12 13	1.7
27	F	07 40	3.4	19 39	3.5	00 45	1.4	13 10	1.6
28	SA	08 28	3.5	20 29	3.6	01 38	1.3	14 00	1.5
29	**SU**	09 10	3.7	21 14	3.7	02 23	1.1	14 43	1.3
30	M	09 48	3.8	21 58	3.9	03 04	1.0	15 24	1.1

Time Zone UT(GMT)

DECEMBER 2009   DUBLIN (NORTH WALL)

HEIGHTS ABOVE CHART DATUM

		High Water				Low Water			
Date		**Morning**		**Afternoon**		**Morning**		**Afternoon**	
		Time	m	Time	m	Time	m	Time	m
1	TU	10 25	4.0	22 41	4.0	03 43	0.9	16 05	0.9
2	W O	11 04	4.1	23 25	4.1	04 22	0.8	16 47	0.7
3	TH	11 45	4.2			05 03	0.7	17 32	0.6
4	F	00 12	4.1	12 31	4.2	05 46	0.8	18 19	0.5
5	SA	01 02	4.1	13 20	4.2	06 33	0.8	19 11	0.6
6	**SU**	01 55	4.0	14 13	4.2	07 24	1.0	20 08	0.6
7	M	02 53	3.9	15 10	4.1	08 21	1.1	21 08	0.7
8	TU	03 55	3.8	16 12	4.0	09 24	1.3	22 11	0.8
9	W ☾	05 01	3.7	17 17	3.9	10 30	1.4	23 16	1.0
10	TH	06 08	3.6	18 25	3.9	11 39	1.4		
11	F	07 14	3.6	19 32	3.8	00 23	1.0	12 49	1.4
12	SA	08 16	3.7	20 36	3.8	01 29	1.1	13 54	1.4
13	**SU**	09 13	3.8	21 36	3.8	02 30	1.1	14 54	1.3
14	M	10 03	3.9	22 28	3.8	03 23	1.1	15 47	1.2
15	TU	10 46	3.9	23 12	3.8	04 08	1.0	16 33	1.1
16	W ●	11 23	4.0	23 49	3.8	04 48	1.0	17 14	1.0
17	TH	11 55	4.0			05 25	1.0	17 52	0.9
18	F	00 22	3.8	12 29	4.0	05 59	1.0	18 29	0.9
19	SA	00 57	3.7	13 04	4.0	06 33	1.1	19 05	0.9
20	**SU**	01 33	3.7	13 41	4.0	07 08	1.1	19 42	1.0
21	M	02 12	3.6	14 21	3.9	07 46	1.2	20 20	1.1
22	TU	02 54	3.5	15 03	3.8	08 27	1.3	21 01	1.1
23	W	03 39	3.4	15 48	3.7	09 13	1.4	21 45	1.2
24	TH ☽	04 29	3.4	16 37	3.6	10 05	1.5	22 35	1.3
25	F	05 26	3.3	17 32	3.5	11 03	1.6	23 32	1.4
26	SA	06 29	3.3	18 33	3.4			12 06	1.6
27	**SU**	07 31	3.4	19 38	3.5	00 35	1.4	13 08	1.6
28	M	08 27	3.5	20 40	3.6	01 36	1.3	14 06	1.4
29	TU	09 17	3.7	21 36	3.8	02 31	1.2	14 59	1.2
30	W	10 04	3.9	22 27	3.9	03 21	1.0	15 48	0.9
31	TH O	10 49	4.1	23 16	4.0	04 08	0.9	16 36	0.6

Time Zone UT(GMT)

KILMORE, CO WEXFORD

The small, picturesque villages of Kilmore and Kilmore Quay are situated in the South East of Wexford, 10 miles from Wexford Town. With miles of beautiful sandy beaches and a stunning marina, the villages are home to many tourists throughout the year. The port of Kilmore Quay is renowned for its history of fishing, commercial and angling. There are numerous charter boats out of Kilmore Quay, drawing anglers from all over the world to its excellent fishing.

Ballyhealy Beach
By Cormac Walsh

Ballyhealy beach is located on the South East coastline of Ireland just east of Kilmore Quay. It is part of a series of different beaches that stretch along the vast coastline from Kilmore Quay to Carnsore point. A short drive from Wexford town and it can be easily accessed from Kilmore Village. Due to its shallow nature it is popular among bathers in the summer months. Over the years, the beach was known for its beautiful soft sand, however, in recent years due to a shift in currents, small rock and stone now covers a lot of the beach.

Past the water's edge, the stone disappears and a shallow sandy seabed extends out to sea dotted with gullies and sandbanks. Tackle losses are rare and a look at low tide will assist the angler in choosing his mark when fishing the high tide. The sea bed is relatively flat, so with a nice southerly or south-westerly breeze at half to low tide, a decent surf is experienced with several surf tables produced.

Tides
The best fishing is usually experienced around half tide to full tide and back down to half tide again. Distance casting is not necessary here; a cast of no more than fifty yards will suffice to get among the fish. At high water the fish tend to come close in to feed around the gullies and sandbanks close to the high water mark.

Species
Ballyhealy, like so many of the south east coast beaches, tends to fish better at night. Fishing can be good all year round with Bass being the most sought after. Other species such as Flounder, Turbot, Tope, Smoothhound, Dogfish and Mackerel are also on offer here. Winter months produce, Bass, Codling, Coalfish and Rockling.

Bait
The baits most commonly used are Lugworm, Ragworm, Mackerel and Peeler Crab. Worm baits tend to produce best results here. However in autumn strips

of fresh Mackerel can be deadly in targeting larger bass. Other tried and tested baits are Sandeel and Squid, but Ragworm definitely holds the honour of being the most successful for most species apart from Dogfish, Smoothhound and Tope for which Mackerel is favoured.

About the Author

The article on Ballyhealy Beach was contributed by Cormac Walsh. Cormac started angling at the age of 6 on the local beaches in Wexford. From the age of 13 he was helping his father Joe with his charter fishing business in Kilmore Quay and at age 18 was skippering charter boats.

Cormac is well respected in angling circles and regularly fishes the east

Cormac with one of many small 2lb Bass (schoolies) to be found amongst the Mackerel in late summer.

and south coastline. He is currently a member of Greystones Ridge SAC.

Tackle and Bait

Murphy's Fishing Tackle Shop
92 North Main Street, Wexford.
Tel: (053) 9124717

'Tackle and bait supplies - Murphy's offer friendly advice, and valuable knowledge on all the local marks and hotspots'

Hayes Cycles	**Dave's Tackle**
108 South Main Street, Wexford.	Ardcavan, Wexford.
Tel: (053) 9122462	Tel: (053) 9124307

WATERVILLE, CO KERRY

Waterville is renowned worldwide for its superb golf courses, its Sea trout, Salmon and Bass angling and its long sandy beaches. The area can boast some of the most spectacular scenery in Kerry and offers walkers, cyclists and anglers endless possibilities for sightseeing, touring and amazing fishing.

Waterville Beach
By Kevin Braine

Waterville beach is located at the village of Waterville in Co Kerry, between Hogs head and Ballyskilligs. The fishing on this beach can be exceptional all year round, and is famous throughout Ireland for its excellent Bass fishing.

The beach is a favourite of many local anglers, especially during the winter months, although the summer months are still very good for lots of species. On this beach there are plenty of Bass between 2lb and 5lb just below the main car park where a lot of anglers fish.

Tides

The best time to fish the beach is from low water up to high on neap tides with good surf, with south to west winds bringing better fishing.

Species

There are many different species to be caught along this beach. Bass are the main target of most; however there is excellent fishing for other species such as Plaice, Flounder, Bull Huss, Dogfish, Ballan Wrasse, Codling, Coalfish, small Turbot and the occasional Mackerel.

Baits

The most commonly used baits here are Crab, Lug worm, Mackerel, Sandeel and Squid, but there is one bait that out fishes any other along here. That is Razor Fish. When the surf is good, I have had most of my Bass on Razor. There are a good few Bass around 8lb to be caught here, the mark sometimes throwing up the odd 12lb Bass every now and again.

Waterville's Kevin Braine with a superb 9 1/2 lb Bass.

About the Author

The article on Waterville Beach was written by Kevin Brain. He has become known as one of the best angling guides in Ireland due to his extensive knowledge of fishing the Kerry area. Kevin's reputation in Ireland has spread beyond our shores, and apart from being the subject of articles in several magazines such as Sea Angler, Total Sea Fishing and other magazines throughout Europe, he was also the guide for Henry Gilby's angling program on Sky Discovery.

Kevin will be releasing a book shortly entitled **'The complete Fishing Book of the South Western Coast of Kerry'**, which will be a must have for all anglers, young and old. The book will detail where to fish, how to get there, what traces and baits to use, the essential information every angler needs for any chance at a successful fishing expedition. Kevin will also be taking over the tackle shop in the village from 01 Jan 09.

Contact information:
More information on the book and details of Kevin's family run angling business can be found at www.kbfishingireland.com or at the below address.

KB Fishing Ireland, Waterville, Co. Kerry
Tel: 00 353 66 9474942
Mobile: 087 6766986
email:info@kbfishingireland.com

Tackle and Bait
Tadhg O'Sullivan Main Street, Waterville, Co. Kerry. Tel: +353 (0)66 9474433 or +353 (0)87 6705121 Email: tadhgosullivanfishingtackle@hotmail.com
Kevin Braine (guide and bait) http://www.kbfishingireland.co.uk/

CLIFDEN, CO GALWAY

Clifden lies about 50 miles northwest of Galway and is the largest town in Connemara. The Great Famine of the 1840's stunted the town's growth, but it has now become a most popular spot for tourists. With its many fine hotels, guesthouses and restaurants, it is the ideal place for holidaymakers. It offers many different activities including mountaineering, walking trails and superb angling.

Steven Turner with a lovely Dab on the rocks at White Lady.

White Lady
By Steven Turner

The beacon tower at Errislannan point is locally known as the 'White Lady' and is becoming popular with sea anglers young and old. Located on the south shore of Clifden bay, the best route to find this mark is to drive from Clifden towards Ballyconneely, and approximately 3.6Km from Clifden there is a sign post for the Alcock and Browne monument pointing to the right up a small road, follow this road for about 5.3Km until you come to a pier, from here you will have to walk, follow the coastline to the north for slightly less than 1Km. For safety I would advise that this be done during the day and returning during daylight hours until you are familiar with the surroundings. A good pair of hiking boots would be a good idea too.

The best fishing is done from the rocks below the beacon into Clifden Bay. Take care while walking on the rocks as they can be very slippery after rain showers.

Tides

Fishing this mark produces well during all stages of the tide for various species, because this is a fairly deep water mark the same tactics can be used at all stages of the tide. For float fishing, a bait can be set up to eight feet from the float as the area is mostly clean bottomed, with the exception of an area of kelp to the north and west of the beacon,. Anglers can fish the bottom to the north west and from low water the north right into the bay, as there are very few obstacles. Distance is not required here, but I would advise the use of grip leads during the tidal flow. One other thing to note, if you are fishing the very low rocks during low tide be observant of the tide and keep an eye behind you, as the tide will cut you off.

Species

This mark holds an excellent array of species; these include Dogfish, Flounder, Dab, Whiting, Codling, Thornback Ray, Blonde Ray, Spotted Ray, Bull Huss, Conger Eel , Ballan Wrasse, Corkwing Wrasse, Pollock, Coalfish, Grey Gurnard, Plaice, Sea Trout and many more.

Bait

The baits most commonly used are Sandeel, Mackerel, Squid, Worm baits can be used to catch flatfish and Wrasse, and even Limpets have been known to be used here for Wrasse. A cocktail of Squid and Mackerel can sometimes out-fish Sandeel when targeting Ray species and float fishing a whole Sandeel along the rocks can often produce large Pollock.

About the Author

The article on White Lady was contributed by Steven Turner. Steven started fishing at the young age of 5 on the North Sea. He moved to Co Galway when he was 8 years old and fished rivers and lakes until 1994. He moved to Salthill in Galway a year later and started taking sea fishing seriously in 1997. Since then Steven has become well known in angling circles all around Ireland.

Steve (left) and Conor Montaine (right) with a brace of Thornback Ray taken at White Lady.

He has been a member of Sea Angling Ireland SAC since 2007 and has also been a member of Galway Bay SAC since 2004. Steve's helpful advice in the Sea Angling Ireland forums and endless knowledge of sea angling has earned him a great reputation as an angler and is well respected by all.

The photographs were provided by Conor Mountaine. Conor is another well known and well respected angler and can be found on many marks in Galway and Wexford

Conor with a 6lb Thorny (Thornback Ray) at White Lady.

Tackle and Bait
Stanley's Fishing Tackle Clifden, Co Galway Tel: (095) 21039 Email: sot@indigo.ie

LOUISBURGH, CO MAYO

Louisburgh is a picturesque little town situated at the mouth of Bunowen River, 16 miles west of Westport. It is a popular spot for couples and families with the romantic solitudes of Glencullin and Doo Lough close by, and an area with fine blue-flagged sandy beaches.

The Old Head at Louisburgh
By Kieran Hanrahan

Probably more famous for the superb views back to Croagh Patrick, the Old Head at Louisburgh offers a wide variety of fishing. The pier is a well-known haunt for both anglers and tourists looking to snap up a few Mackerel around high water. Inside it lies a small and calm sandy beach with little in the way of currents and the odd snag near the harbour. There are no Conger eels here as the harbour often dries out at low water. Terns routinely pluck Sandeels and Sprat from these sheltered waters and Mullet will often shoal here especially at low water. Rougher ground extends out on the coast heading west; with sand invading gullies to give excellent cover for small fish and crustaceans. A track from near the pier up through the old oak forest will bring you to several grassy platforms with a rocky margin on the far western side. Casting any distance will land you onto sand although you can float fish the weedy rough ground margins as well. Many anglers fish one rod at distance and one close in.

Tides

The pier fishing is usually done approaching high tide, and since the beach is very shallow, unless you are targeting the Mullet, it is best left until darkness. Weavers are a common by-catch here so some care must be taken if you catch anything that looks like a small whiting. On the western rock marks, fishing can be done at any time.

Species

Numerous species are caught here every year, with the pier mostly reserved for the Mackerel bashers! This said it has produced Thornback rays on the seaward side and flatfish as well as Mullet inside the harbour. On the rock marks, Flounder and Dabs are the main target, with Thornbacks also taken and Dogfish common all year. The summer brings in Mackerel, Scad, Launce, the occasional Sea Trout and smallish Pollack to spinning tactics. Conger eels and Wrasse are found in the weedy margins. If you follow the path west to some severe rocks, there are Triggerfish in the coves. Coalfish replace the Pollack in winter as do Rockling the Wrasse, with Whiting also a possibility in calm weather. The Clew Bay Skate migrate past here in late autumn, as evident by the many charter boats stationed no more than 300 yards offshore.

Bait

The baits most commonly used are Lugworm and Mackerel. Other tried and tested baits are Sandeel and Squid, the former essential for fishing off the beach. Bread and small white flies will take the Mullet and the latter accounts for the odd Sea Trout. The best lures are German Sprats and Flying Cs for the Pollack, and there are even a few unconfirmed reports of Bass falling to poppers at dusk in the sand filled gullies.

About the Author

The article on the old head in Louisburgh was written by Kieran Hanrahan. Kieran started fishing at age six in the rock pools in Lahinch, using roach hooks to pull out strap conger eels and blennies. His theory was that when he moved west ten years ago he would get to do loads of fishing... but a small and growing family somehow intervened! This said his eldest lad is now eight and very keen so he now has a perfect excuse for dodging off at weekends more often.

The Old Head looking east towards Croagh Patrick.

"Stalking fish with a light spinning rod and belly pack over Mayo's unending and virgin rocky ground is my favourite pursuit. I have fished in places that have never seen an angler and the quality of the fishing can be breathtaking. People have been very generous with their marks too... I've been a contributing writer to the Irish Angler magazine since it was founded by DHP and Roger many years ago and now work with David Dinsmore on the Species File and Around Ireland pieces. My work has taken me all over the country for the last twenty years, so I have a pretty good knowledge of sea angling around Ireland but it has also been a great excuse to link up with people and learning all about their area. I've learned a great deal by listening to experienced "local" anglers..." Kieran Hanrahan

Tackle and Bait

Westport Marine Supplies Ltd.
Shop Street, Westport, Co. Mayo.
Tel: (098) 28800

BUNCRANA, CO DONEGAL

The main town and resort on the lovely Inishowen Peninsula, Buncrana boasts a 3 mile sandy beach. Buncrana's Irish name means "Foot of the River" and one of its many beautiful features is the walk under beech, maple and lime trees beside the brown waters of the River Crana. The Crana River is renowned for its Salmon angling and it adorns Swan Park.

Don Browse battles with a Tope on Fahan Beach.

Fahan Beach
By Don Browse

Fahan Beach is located just a few miles from Buncrana in Co Donegal and is just a ten minute drive from Derry. It is surrounded by wonderful scenery with a beautiful view of Lough Swilly. The main fishing mark on this beach is just a few minutes' walk down from the right hand side of the marina.

Tides

If fishing this mark I would recommend using grip leads as there can be a very strong current when the tide is turning. Most experienced anglers that fish this mark would normally fish the last 3 1/2 to 4 hours of the out-going tide, down to low water, and an hour or so into the rise. At the start of the session distance casting may be required, as this is a fairly shallow beach, but off shore there is a deep channel.

Species

There is a mix of species to be caught from this beach. As always you will get Dogfish and in the winter months you will get the Whiting, but when the seasons change from winter to spring, and march finally arrives, this beach comes alive with the appearance of Thornback Rays. Many other species will be caught here also include Red and Tub Gurnard, Dab, small Turbot and the occasional Sea Trout.

Baits

Any of the usual baits work well off this beach. For Dabs and Turbot, Lugworm and Ragworm are the norm. Large strips of Mackerel are very effective for catching dogfish while Sandeels and Sprats (white bait) prove to be very successful for tempting the Sea Trout. Small pieces of mackerel prove to be a top bait for Gurnards but the main species from this beach is the Thornback Ray. Mackerel, Sandeel and Squid are the most common baits used. On this beach the Ray average from 3lb to 6lb but a lot of 8lb and 12lb fish have been caught here with one in August caught weighing 16lb 3oz, which was returned safely back to the water.

Rigs

Any of the usual rigs work from this beach, though the pulley rig is the most favoured as distance casting is needed at the start of your session. Beachcaster rods and multiplier reels are the normal set up as the added distance is sometimes required but fixed spool reels are also used. I personally fish with good carp rods of 13 foot length and a multiplier loaded with 18lb line with a 50lb shock leader.

About the Author

The article on Fahan Beach was contributed by Don Browse. Don lives in Derry City although the bulk of his fishing is done around Donegal. He likes to fish a diverse range of marks on rocks, piers and beaches. He can also be found regularly fishing in his local river, River Foyle, which is known for its Sea Trout and Mullet and Pike fishing on the lakes around Derry.

Don with a thornback Ray on Fahan Beach.

Don has been fishing for the past 41 years after being introduced to it at the age of 5 by his grandfather and uncle. Don is, not only a keen Sea Angler, but regularly fly fishes for trout and salmon

Tackle and Bait
Buncrana Anglers Association Angling Centre, Castle Lane, Buncrana, Co. Donegal. Tel: (074) 9363733

BRITTAS BAY, CO WICKLOW

Brittas Bay boasts 4 miles of beautiful white sand dunes and clean beaches. The beach at Brittas bay has won a European Union (EU) Blue Flag - the international emblem for the highest quality beach areas in Europe - for five consecutive years. With no headlands to interfere with the peaceful rhythm, it is ideal for bathing, sailing and walking.

Ennereilly Beach
By Roger O Bogaigh

Ennereilly Beach is situated south of Brittas Bay and is a mark that can fish well in summer and winter with dawn and dusk coinciding with high water giving best results. Firstly how to access the mark. From Dublin take the N11 as far as the crossroads after Jack Whites pub and turn left down a very twisty road, you will then come to a T junction, turn right and follow the road until you come to another T junction you can park here and you will notice a turn stile and some conifers. This gives access to a nice stroll over the sand dunes (three very large ones) so travel light for this area. Alternatively if you turn right at the second T junction and follow the coast road you will come across a small car park on your left. Park here and walk back to a laneway which leads to the beach it has a black and yellow barrier to keep cars out. Another option would be to carry on further down this road to Pennycomequick Bridge (parking here is limited to say the least) if you climb over the gate simply follow the river till you reach the beach. Lastly slightly further on down the road is a small parking area that gives instant access to the beach

Species
Species available are normally Cod, Whiting and Flounder during winter with the chance of a Bass if it stays mild, possibly until mid-November some years. Summer species include Bass, Smoothhound (starry and common), Tope, Flounder, Ray, the beloved Dogfish and the odd Sea Trout (for which a licence is required). This beach can throw up the odd surprise and with sea temperatures rising who knows! Several Trigger fish washed ashore in late autumn last year though there are no reports of a hook up yet!

Bait and Rigs
For winter fishing I wouldn't visit this beach without Lugworm, Squid or Mackerel. For summer fishing Lug, Rag, Crab, Mackerel and Sandeel will all produce. Sandeel is a must if targeting Ray.

Rigs to try would be three hook flappers for close in work; two hook clipped down for Cod and pulley rigs (plain or panelled) for Ray and Bass. One thing to remember with this mark is to start in close and increase distance until you find the fish, as normally due to the depth of water most fish feed quite close in. I've had Smoothhound on Ragworm 30 feet out on a sunny morning!

Tips
In general this is not a snaggy beach besides two spots, one at the first car park directly in front of you as you enter the beach; don't fish the first 100 yards or you will lose gear The second is directly in line with the river at Pennycomequick Bridge. Just keep to the right of it as its very rough and a tackle graveyard maybe the spot to try with a plug or spinner.

About the Author

The article on Ennereilly Beach was written by Roger O'Bogaigh. Roger, a fishaholic, can be found on a beach between Dundalk and Waterford at least once a week.

Originally from Manchester, Roger moved to New Zealand where he started fishing from the early age of 6. He moved to

Roger O Bogaigh with a beautiful 11lb 1oz Bass.

Ireland at age 11 and has lived in the Greystones/Bray area for the last 32 years.

Roger is well known and respected in angling circles throughout Ireland and is currently a Sea Angling Ireland SAC member.

Tackle and Bait
Avonmore Tackle Products Pat Cullen, 36 main Street, Rathdrum, Co. Wicklow . Tel: (0404) 43142
Dogs, Rods and Guns South Quay, Wicklow Town, Co. Wicklow. Tel: (0404) 25558 Web: www.dogsrodsguns.com

Antrim

Antrim Country Sports and Tackle
9 Rough Lane, Larne, Co. Antrm.
Tel: +44 28 9446 7378

C F Beattie
39 Main Street, Ballycarry, Co.
Antrim.
Tel: +44 28 9335 3462

R Bell
40 Ann Street, Ballycastle, Co.
Antrim.
Tel: +44 28 2076 2520

McCroggan's Fishing Tackle
34 Broughshane Street, Ballymena,
Co. Antrim.
Tel: +44 28 2564 6370

E J Cassells
43 Main Street, Ballymoney, Co.
Antrim.
Tel: +44 28 2766 3216

Smyth's Tackle
17 Enagh Road, Ballymoney, Co.
Antrim.
Tel: +44 28 2766 4259

Joseph Braddell & Son Ltd
11 North Street, Belfast, Co Antrim.
BT1 1NA
Tel: +44 28 90320525 Fax: +44 28
90322657
Web: www.braddells.co.uk

Gone Fishin
29 North Street, Carrickfergus, Co
Antrim, BT38 7AQ
Tel: +44 28 93 367082 Web:
www.creativelivingni.com

Red Bay Boats
Coast Roar, Cushedall, Co. Antrim.
Tel: +44 28 2177 1331

Larne Angling Centre
128 Main Street, Larne, Co. Antrim.
Tel: +44 28 2827 0404

L&G Tackle
50 Waterfall Road, Gleno, Larne, Co.
ANtirm
Tel: Graeme at + 44 7801782447 or
+ 44 28 28275626 or Liam at + 44
7867722971

**Lisburn Sports Centre, Guns &
Tackle**
9 Smithfield Square, Lisburn, co.
Antrim.
Tel: +44 28 9267 7975

R Mc Knight Jewellers
Main Street, Portglenone, Co.
Antrim.
Tel: +44 28 2582 2269

J S Mullan
74 Main Street, Portrush, Co. Antrim.
Tel: +44 28 7082 2209

Armagh

Stinson The Saddler
20 Thomas Street, Armagh
Tel: +44 28 3752 3339

G.I Stores
5 Dobbin Street, Armagh, Co.
Armagh bt61 7qq
Tel: 02837522335 Web:
www.gistores.com

Outdoor Experience
29/31 Castle Street, Portadown,
CRAIGAVON, Armagh. BT62 1BA
Tel: +44 28 38339333

Premier Angling Centre
17 Queen Street, Lurgan,Co Armagh.
Tel: +44 28 3832 5204

Willis Hardware
88 Main Street, Markethill, Co.
Armagh.
Tel: +44 28 3755 1245

Carlow

Carlow Coarse Angling Supplies
8 St. Fiacc's Terrace, Graiguecullen,
Carlow, Co. Carlow.
Tel: 05991 37664 or 087 2257452
E-Mail: gerrymcstraw@yahoo.ie or
carlowcoarseangling@hotmail.com
Web: www.carlowcoarseanglingsup-
plies.com

M A McCullagh
Market Square, Muine Bheag, Co.
Carlow.
Tel: (059) 9721381 Fax: (059)
9721381

Murph's Fishing
Tullow Street, Carlow Town.
Tel: (059) 9132839

Liam O' Connor
O' Connor's Newsagents, The
Square, Tullow, Co. Carlow.
Tel: (059) 9151337

Cavan

Aim and Swing
Killyfassey, Mountnugent, Co. Cavan.
Tel: (049) 8540131 or (087) 2750826
Fax: (049) 8540995

Spinners
Main St, Killeshandra, Co. Cavan.
Tel: (049) 436 3877

Joe Mulligan
Main St, Shercock, Co. Cavan.
Tel: (042) 9669184

Sports World
Townhall Street, Cavan.
Tel: (049) 4331812

Sheelin Shamrock Hotel
Mountnugent, Lough Sheelin, Co.
Cavan.
Tel: (049) 8540113

Philip Smith
Lavagh, Kilnaleck, Lough Sheelin,
Co. Cavan.
Tel: (049) 4336156

Clare

Patrick Cleary
Westcliffe Lodge, Spanish Point, Co.
Clare.
Tel: (065) 7084037

Joe O'Loughlin
Main Street, Lisdoonvarna, Co. Clare.
Tel: (065) 7074038

Michael O'Sullivan
50 Moore Street, Kilrush, Co. Clare.
Tel: (065) 9051071

Bourkes Fishing Tackle Shop
Kilrush Road, Kilkee, Co. Clare.
Tel: +353 (0)65 9056363
Email: fishing@westclare.net Web:
www.fishing.westclare.net

Siopa Fán óir
Shop and Post Office, Craggagh,
Fanore, County Clare.
Tel: (065) 7076131 Email:
shop@fanore.com

Riverbank Fishing Shop
Main Street, Sixmilebridge, Co. Clare.
Tel: (061) 369633

Tierneys cycles& fishing
17Abbey Street, Ennis, Co Clare.
Tel: (065) 6829433

Cork

Jeffersports
7 Pearse St., Bandon, Co. Cork.
Tel: (023) 41133
Email: jefsport@indigo.ie

Ballyhass Lakes
Trout Fishing and Holiday Homes
Cecilstown, Mallow County Cork Ireland
Tel: + 353 22 277732 Fax
E Mail: info@ballyhasslakes.ie Web:
www.ballyhasslakes.ie

Clontackle and Leisure
2 Pearse Street, Clonakilty,Co. Cork
Tel: (023) 35580 or (086) 3620349
Email: clontackle@hotmail.com Web:
www.clontackle.com

Country Lifestyle
Unit C, Spa Square, Mallow, Co. Cork
Tel: (022) 20121 Fax: (022) 20104
Email: contrylifestyle@eircom.net

Cobh Fishing Tackle
Sycamore House, Ballynoe, Cobh,
Co. Cork.
Tel: (021) 4812167
Email: seaangling@esatclear.ie Web:
http://www.seafishing.irl.com/

Cork Angling and Outdoor Centre
Kinsale Road Business Park, Kinsale
Road Roudabout, Cork.
Tel: (021) 432 1000
Web: www.corkanglingdirect.com

Halfway Angling Centre
Halfway Angling Centre, Halfway,
Ballinhassig, Co. Cork.
Tel: (021) 4885894
Web:
http://www.tackledirectireland.com

The Hire Shop
8 Main Street, Kinsale, Co. Cork.
Tel: (021) 4774884
Email: info@thehireshopirl.com

T.W. Murray& Co Ltd
87 Patrick St, Cork.
Tel: (021) 4271089

Rivers Edge Tackle
Inniscarra Road, Carrigrohane, Co.
Cork.
Tel: (021) 4871771

T. H. Sports Ltd
Main Street, Midleton, Co. Cork.
Tel: (021) 4631800

Bait All Tackle
1 Richmond Hill, Fermoy, Co.Cork.
Tel: (025) 33361

Derry

Hueston's
55 Main Street, Castledawson, Co.
Derry.
Tel: +44 28 7966 8282

Moorebrook lodge
46 Glebe Road, Castlerock, Coleraine,
Co. Derry.
Tel: +44 28 7084 9408

Rod & Line
1 Clarendon Street, Derry.
Tel: +44 28 7126 2877

Glenowen Fisheries
Creggan Coutry Park, Westway, BT48
9NU.
Tel: +44 28 7137 1544

S J Mitchell & Co
29 Main Street, Limavady, Co Derry.
Tel: +44 28 7772 2128

Donegal

Buncrana Anglers Association
Angling Centre, Castle Lane,
Buncrana, Co. Donegal.
Tel: (074) 9363733

Charles Bonner
The Bridge, Dungloe, Co. Donegal.
Tel: (074) 95 21163

Charlie Doherty
Main St, Donegal.
Tel: (074) 97 21119

Lough Swilly Flies & Angling Centre
Roughpark, Ramelton Road,
Letterkenny, Co. Donegal.
Tel: (074) 9168496
Email: jmclswillyflies@eircom.net

Top Tackle
55 Port Road, Letterkenny, Co.Donegal.
Tel: (074) 9167545
Email: toptackle@gmail.com

Down

Angus Cochrane
The Harbour, Ardglass, Co. Down.
Tel: +44 28 4484 1551

Charles Mulhall
1 Quay Street, Ardglass, Co. Down.
Tel: +44 28 4484 1301

Dairy Fishery & Tackle Shop
179a Belfast Road, Ballynahinch, Co. Down.
Tel: +44 28 9756 3380

The Tackle Shop
Old Mill, Ballydown Road,
Banbridge, Co. Down.
Tel: +44 28 4062 2226

McKees Fishing Tackle
59 Church Street, Bangor, Co. Down.
Tel: +44 28 9141 4983

Trap & Tackle
6 Seacliff Road, Bangor, Co. Down.
Tel: +44 28 9145 8515

Tight Lines
198-200 Albert Bridge Road, Belfast, Co. Down.
Tel: +44 28 9045 7357

Belfast Angling Centre
34 York Road, Belfast , Co. Down.
Tel: +44 28 90747074
www.belfastanglingcentre.com

The Village Tackle Shop
55a Newtownbreda Road, Newtownbreda, Co. Down.
Tel: +44 28 90 491916

Comber Angling & Country Pursuits
23 Bridge Street, Comber, Co. Down.
Tel: +44 28 9187 0777

J Graham & Sons
47 Greencastle St, Kilkeel, Co Down.
Tel: +44 28 4176 2777

McConnell & Hanna
19 Newcastle St, Kilkeel, Co Down.
Tel: +44 28 4176 2226

Jack's Angling
Unit 1F, Altona Business Park, Lisburn City, Co., Down. BT3755QB
Tel: +44 28 9267 6300.

Four Seasons
47 Main Street, Newcastle, Co Down.
Tel: +44 28 4372 5078

Jack Smyth Angling & Outdoors
5-9 Kildare Street, Newry, Co. Down.
Tel: +44 28 3026 5303

Mourne Valley Tackle
50 Main Street, Newtownards, Co. Down.
Tel: +44 28 8166 1543

Dublin

A B C Fishing Tackle Specialists
15 Mary's Abbey, Dublin 7.
Tel: (01) 8731525

Angling & Shooting Centre
Ballydowd, Lucan, Co. Dublin.
Tel: (01) 6281112

Baumann's
Old Dublin Road, Stillorgan, Co. Dublin.
Tel: (01) 2884021 Fax: (01) 2881637
Email: info@baumanns.ie Web: www.baumanns.ie

Boland's Hardware
349 Ballyfermot Rd, Ballyfermot, Dublin 10.
Tel: (01) 6264777 Fax: (01) 6231911

Patrick Cleere & Son Ltd
Unit 16B, Kilcock Rd, Clane, Co Kildare
Tel: (045)893551

Andrew Boyce Bait Shop
80 Rathsallagh Park, Shankill, Co Dublin. Tel 085 1006207

Henry's Tackle Shop
19 Ballybough Road, Dublin 3
Tel: (01) 8555216 Fax: (01) 8555218
Email: henrystackleshop@eircom.net
Web:
http://www.henrystackleshop.com/

Mulhuddart Angling Supplies
Unit 3a, Mulhuddart Village, Dublin 15
Tel: +353 (86) 2439594

Rory's Fishing Tackle
17a Temple Bar, Dublin 2
Tel: (01) 6772351 Fax: (01) 6719986
E-mail: sales@rorys.ie Web:
www.rorys.ie

Southside Angling
Cork Street, Dublin 8
Tel: (01) 4530266
Email: southsideangling@eircom.net

Tallaght Rod & Gun Shop
Unit 2 Castletymon S.C., Tallaght,
Dublin 24.
Tel: (01) 4526522

Fermanagh

Benny B Stuart
68 Main Street, Ballinamallard, Co
Fermanagh.
Tel: +44 28 6638 1321.

Mickey McGrath
Carlton Park Fishing Centre.
Tel: +44 28 6865 8181

Cloughballymill Angling Centre
Unit 3, Sligo Road, Enniskillen. BT74
7JY
Tel: +44 28 6632 2008

Frankie McPhillips
The Butter Market, Enniskillen, Co.
Fermanagh.
Tel: +44 28 6632 3047

Home, Field & Stream
18 Church Street, Enniskillen, Co.
Fermanagh.
Tel: +44 28 6632 2114
Web: www.homefieldandstream.com

Mullin's
Sligo Road, Enniskillen, Co.
Fermanagh.
Tel: + 44 28 6632 4975

John E Richardson
9 East Bridge Street, Enniskillen, Co.
Fermanagh.
Tel: +44 28 6632 2608.

John Ruddy
Castle Street, Irvinestown, Co. Fer-
managh.
Tel: +44 28 68621247.

Country Sports
52 Drumadravy Road, Irvinestown,
Co. Fermanagh.
Tel: +44 28 6862 1788

F A Moffitt
Main Street, Kesh, Co. Fermanagh
Tel: +44 28 6863 1091

Palm Bush Filling Station
Letterkeen, Co Fermanagh.
Tel: +44 28 6863 1696

Castle Marine
Castle Archdale Country Park, Co
Fermanagh.
Tel: +44 28 6862 8097

Erne Tackle
118 Main Street, Lisnaskea, Co. Fermanagh.
Tel: +44 28 6772 1969

Galway

Corrib Tackle
2 Kilkerrin Park, Liosban Industrial
Estate, Galway.
Tel: (091) 769974
Email: ferrox@eircom.net Web:
www.corribtackle.com

Cong Angling Center
Cong, Co, Mayo
Tel: (094) 9546848 or 087 9096086
Email:conganglingcenter@eircom.net

Duffy's Tackle Shop
5 Mainguard St, Galway.
Tel: (091) 562367
Email: duffyb@eircom.net

K. Duffy's Fishing
Main Street, Headford, Co. Galway
Tel: (093) 35449
Email: paul@kduffy.com

Freeney's
High St, Galway.
Tel: (091) 568794

Anne Kyne
Clonbur, Co. Galway.
Tel: (094) 954 6197

Thomas Tuck
Oughterard, Co. Galway.
Tel: (091) 552335 Fax: (091) 552335
Email: tucksfishingtackle@eircom.net

Stanley's Fishing Tackle
Clifden, Co. Galway.
Tel: (095) 21039
Email: sot@indigo.ie

Kerry

Jim Halpin Shooting Supplies
William Street, Listowel, Co. Kerry.
Tel: +353 (0)68 22392
Email: info@halpins.net Web:
www.halpins.net

Killarney Fishing Center
3 Glebe Lane, Killarney, Co. Kerry.
Tel: +353 (0)64 22884 or +353 (0)86
8435028 Fax: +353 (0)64 22884
Email: johnbuckley17@eircom.net
Web: www.killarneyflyfishing.com

Landers Outdoor World
Mile Height, Tralee, Co. Kerry
Tel: +353 (0)66 712 6644 or +353
(0)87 219 0930 Fax: +353 (0)66 712
4378
Email: info@landers.ie Web:
www.landers.ie

Tadhg O'Sullivan
Main Street, Waterville, Co. Kerry.
Tel: +353 (0)66 9474433 or +353
(0)87 6705121
Email:
tadhgosullivanfishingtackle@hotmail.
com

O'Neills
6 Plunkett Street, Killarney, Co.
Kerry.
Tel: +353 (0)64 31970 Fax: +353
(0)64 35689

Kildare

Cleere's Angling Centre
Unit 16B, Clane Business Park, Kil-
cock Road, Clane, Co. Kildare.
Tel: +353 (0)45 893551
E:sales@fishingirelandcentre.com
Web: www.fishingirelandcentre.com

Countryman Angling
Leanne House, Pacelli Road, Naas,
Co. Kildare.
Tel: +353 (0)45 879341
E: countryman_angling@iolfree.ie

Newbridge Garden Centre
Moorefield Road, Newbridge, Co.Kil-
dare.
Tel: +353 (0)45 431028
Email: laurageorge.egan@gmail.com

Griffin Hawe Ltd
22 Duke Street, Athy, Co. Kildare.
Tel: +353 (0)59 8631221 Fax: +353
(0)59 8638885
Email: johnbutler@griffenhawe.ie
Web: http://www.griffinhawe.ie/

M.A. Finlay
Rathangan Road, Monasterevin, Co.
Kildare.
Tel: +353 (0)45 525331 or +353
(0)86 4040809 Fax: +353 (0)45
525184
Email: mafinlay@eircom.net

Kilkenny

Town & County Sports Shop
82 High Street, Kilkenny.
Tel: (056) 7721517 Fax: (056)
7767922

Laois

Irish Fly Craft
Abbeyleix, Co Laois, Ireland.
Tel: +353 (0)86 8451257
E-mail: irishflycraft@eircom.net
Web: www.irishflycraft.com

Laois Fishing Supplies
Ballybrittas, Portlaoise, Co. Laois.
Tel: +353 (0)57 8633923
E-mail:
info@laoisfishingsupplies@eircom.n
et Web: www.laoisfishingsupplies.com

The Tackle Shop
Maura Kelly, The Tackle Shop,
Mountrath, Co.Laois .
Tel: +353 (0)57 8732162

Leitrim

Tooman Angling & Leisure
Bridge Street, Carrick on Shannon,
Co. Leitrim.
Tel: +353 (0)71 9621872

The Waterfront Bait and Tackle
Kilclare, Carrick on Shannon, Co.
Leitrim.
Tel: +353 (0)71 9641599 or +353
(0)87 9647303
Email: stefan.hoare@yahoo.com

Limerick

Bonds Tackle
40 Wickham St, Limerick.
Tel: +353 (0)61 316809 Fax: +353
(0)61 473017

**The Fishing Shooting Archery
Store**
The Milk Market, Ellen Street, Limerick.
Tel: +353 (0)61 413484
Email: steve74@gofree.indigo.ie
Web: www.flyfish.ie

The Shoe Shop
New Street, Abbeyfeale, Co. Limerick
Tel: +353(0)68 31411

Pet Barn
Bishops Street, Newcastle West,Co.
Limerick.
Tel: +353 (0)69 61877

The County Dresser
Station Road, Adare, Co. Limerick.
Tel: +353 (0)61 396915

Kingfisher Angling Centre
Castleconnell, Co. Limerick.
Tel: +353 (0)61 377407 or +353
(0)87 2922413
Email: paddyguerin@eircom.net
Web:
www.ireland360.com/kingfisher/

Longford

Edward Denniston & Co
Centenary Square, Longford.
Tel: +353 (0)43 46345

J & B Holmes
Main Street, Lanesboro, Co. Longford.
Tel: +353 (0)43 21491

Louth

Drogheda Angling Centre
Fairgreen, Drogheda, Co. Louth.
Tel: (041) 9845442

Island Fishing Tackle & Firearms
58 Park St, Dundalk, Co. Louth.
Tel: (042) 9335698 Fax: (042)
9335698
Email: islandtackle@eircom.net

Euro Tackle
Unit 11,Demesne Shopping
Centre,Dundalk Co.Louth.
Tel: (042) 9327623
Web: www.euro-tackle.com Email:
eurotackle@yahoo.ie

Greenore Co-op
22 Euston St, Greenore, Louth, Ireland.
Tel: +353 (0)42 937 3822 or +353
(0)87 2620174
Email: eurotackle@yahoo.ie

Mayo

Ballina Angling Centre
Dillon Terrace, Ballina, Co. Mayo.
Tel: (096) 21850 Fax: (096) 21850
Email: Michael@BallinaAnglingCentre.com Web:
http://ww.ballinaanglingcentre.com

Cong Angling Centre
Cong, Co, Mayo
Tel: (094) 9546848 or 087 9096086
Email:conganglingcenter@eircom.net

Seamus Boland
Bridge Street, Swinford, Co. Mayo.
Tel: 094 9251149 Fax: 094 9251149
Email: julieboland4553@hotmail.com

Billy Bourke's Outdoor Pursuits
Ballinrobe, Co. Mayo.
Tel: (092) 41262

Christy Murphy Angling Centre
Linenhall Street, Castlebar, Co. Mayo.
Tel: (087) 2994217

Erris Autoparts & Accessories
Belmullet, Co. Mayo.
Tel: (097) 82093

Field and Stream
Main Street, Castlebar, Co. Mayo.
Tel: (094) 21030

Hewetson's
Bridge Street, Westport, Co. Mayo.
Tel: (098) 26018 Fax: (098) 27075

Dermot O'Connor's Fishing Tackle shop
Ballinrobe, Co. Mayo.
Tel: (092) 41083 Fax: (096) 21850

Fred O'Connor
Cong, Co. Mayo.
Tel: (092) 46008 Fax: (092) 46771

Cong Angling Centre
Cong, Co. Mayo.
Tel: (094) 9546848 (087) 9096086

Ridge Pool Tackle Shop
Cathedral Road, Ballina, Co. Mayo.
Tel: (096) 72656

Sportfish Tackle Shop
Ridgepool Road, Ballina, Co. Mayo.
Tel: (096) 74455

PJ Tiernan
Foxford, Co. Mayo.
Tel: (094) 56731 Fax: (094) 56731
Email: tiernanbros@eircom.net Web:
http://www.tiernanbrothers.8k.com/

Rod Tye
Cushlough, Ballinrobe, Co Mayo
Tel: (094) 9542374
Email: rodtye@eircom.net Web:
www.rodtye.ie

Westport Marine Supplies Ltd.
Shop Street, Westport, Co. Mayo.
Tel: (098) 28800

John Walkin's Fishing Tackle Shop
Market Square, Ballina, Co. Mayo.
Tel: (096) 22442 or (087) 2959225
Fax: (096) 22442

Monaghan

Tackleshop
Main Street, Castleblaney, Monaghan.
Tel: 087 9394990 or 087 2852646

M.C. Graham
Old Cross Square, Monaghan.
Tel: (047) 71453

Venture Sports Equipment
71A Glaslough Street, Monaghan.
Tel: (047) 81495 Fax: (047) 81495
Email: venturesports@monaghan-outdoors.com Web:
www.monaghan-outdoors.com

Offaly

Killeens Village Tavern
Shannonbridge.
Tel: +353 (0)90 9674112
Email: derry.killeen@gmail.com

The Tackle Shop
Rahan, Tullamore, Co. Offaly.
Tel: +353 (0)57 9355979
Email: grif@eircom.net

The Old Forge
West End, Banagher, Co. Offaly.
Tel: +353 (0)57 9151504
Email: kmduthie2@eircom.net

Alo Moran
Shannonbridge, Co. Offaly.
Tel: +353 (0)90 9674124

Roscommon

Angling Supplies
Henry Street, Roscommon, Co.
Roscommon.
Tel: (0906) 628958 Email: anglingsupplies@eircom.net

Christopher Wynne
Main Street, Boyle, Co. Roscommon.
Tel: (079) 62456

Abbey Marine and Fieldsports
Carrick Road, Boyle, Co.
Roscommon.
Tel: (071) 9663532

John Hunt
Castlerae, Co. Roscommon.
Tel: (0907) 20111

Sligo

Barton Smith
Hyde Bridge, Sligo.
Tel: (071) 46111 Fax: (071) 44196

Kingfisher Bates
Pier Road, Enniscrone, Co. Sligo.
Tel: (096) 36733

Brid Mc Elgunn
Carrownacleiga, Coolaney, Sligo, Co.
Sligo.
Tel: (071) 30512

Tipperary

Premier Marine
Main Street, Littleton, Thurles,
Co.Tipperary.
Tel: (0504) 44336

Kavanagh's Sports Shop
Upper O' Connell Street, Clonmel,
Co. Tipperary.
Tel: (052) 21279

Open Season
55 Kenyon St, Nenagh, Co. Tipperary.
Tel: (067) 31774

JJ Percival
Castle St, Roscrea, Co. Tipperary.
Tel: (0505) 21586

FishHunt
Philip Maher, Fishhunt, Touraneena, Ballinamult, Clonmel, Co. Tipperary.
Tel: 058 47524 Mobile: 087 8399345
Email: fishhunt@indigo.ie

TJs Angling Centre
Main St, Ballina, Killaloe, Co. Tipperary.
Tel: 061 61 376009 Fax: 061 61 375556
Email: info@tjsangling.com Web: www.tjsangling.com

Garrykennedy Angling Supplies - Pike and perch lures
Garranmore, Newtown , Nenagh, Co. Tipperary
Email: mroll@iol.ie

Clonanav Angling Centre
Clonanav Farmhouse, Ballymacarbry, via Clonmel, Co. Waterford.
Tel: (052) 36765
Email: andrew@flyfishingireland
Web: www.flyfishingireland.com

Tyrone

Loughview Worms
Eamon O'Hagan, 78a Aneeter Road, Coagh, Cookstown,TyroneBT800HZ
Tel: +44 28 8673 5893 or +44 7980 60745
email: eamonohagan@btinternet.com

S Quinn & Sons
Main Street, Coalisland, Co. Tyrone.
Tel: +44 28 8774 0308

Cahoon Bros.
2 Irish Street, Dungannon, Co. Tyrone.
Tel: +44 28 8772 2754

C A Anderson & Co.
64 Market Street, Omagh, Co. Tyrone.
Tel: +44 28 8224 2311

D Floyd
28 Melmount Villas, Strabane, Co. Tyrone.
Tel: +44 28 7188 3981

Divers Shop
5 Castle Street, Strabane, Co. Tyrone.
Tel: +44 28 7188 3021

Waterford

Army & Outdoor Stores
New St, Waterford.
Tel: (051) 857554 Fax: (051) 383243
Email: nmcdonagh@eircom.net

Angling and Outdoor Centre
Westgate Retail Park, Tramore Road, Waterford.
Tel: (051) 844314 Fax: (051) 844314
Email: bait@eircom.net

Baumann
Watchmakers, Jewellers and Fishing
Tackle
6 St Mary St, Dungarvan, Waterford
Tel: (058) 41395
Email: baumann@cablesurf.com

Blackwater Lodge Salmon Fishery
Blackwater Lodge, Upper Ballyduff,
County Waterford.
Tel: +353 58 60235
E-mail: info@ireland-salmon-
fishing.net Website:
www.ireland-salmon-fishing.net

Clonanav Angling Centre
Clonanav Farmhouse, Ballymacarbry,
via Clonmel, Co. Waterford.
Tel: (052) 36765
Email: andrew@flyfishingireland
Web: www.flyfishingireland.com

Dingleys
 [Also sells fresh sandwiches. Open
Sunday]
Units 3&4 Dock Road, Dunmore
East, Waterford.

Shoot'n & Fish'n
26A Ballybricken, Waterford.
Tel: (051) 878007

Titelines Tackle Shop
Main Street, Cappoquin, Co Water-
ford.
Tel: (058) 54152

Map and Compass
5 Gladstone Street , Waterford City,
Co Waterford.
Tel: +353 (0)51877713

Westmeath

Geraldine Clarke
Finae, Lough Sheelin, Co. Westmeath.
Tel: (043) 81158

Lough Ree Active
The Derries, Ballykeeran, Athlone ,o.
Westmeath.
Tel: (090) 6491966
Web: http://www.lractive.com/

David O'Malley
33 Dominick Street, Mullingar, Co.
Westmeath.
Tel: (044) 48300
Email: dpomalley@eircom.net

Scully Guns and Tackle
Hudson Bay, Athlone, Co.
Westmeath.
Tel: (0902) 92486

Strand Fishing Tackle
Strand, Athlone, Co. Westmeath.
Tel: (086) 8254141 Fax: (0902) 79277
Email: powell@iol.ie

Wexford

Murphy's Fishing Tackle Shop
92 North Main Street, Wexford.
Tel: (053) 9124717

Hayes Cycles
108 South Main Street, Wexford.
Tel: (053) 9122462

Danny's Bait and Tackle
St Senan's Rd ,Enniscorthy, Wexford.
Tel: (053) 9243571

Fishing Center Bass
28 Fairfields Close, Adamstown,
Co.Wexford, Ireland.
Tel: (083) 3546602
ww.fishing-center-bass.com

Wicklow

Avonmore Tackle Products
Pat Cullen, 36 main Street, Rathdrum,
Co. Wicklow .
Tel: (0404) 43142

Charles Camping
Blessington, Co. Wicklow.
Tel: (045) 865351 Fax: (045) 891183

The Outpost
Edward Street, Baltinglass, Co Wick-
low.
Tel: 059 6482876 or 087 2401173

Viking Tackle Bray
79 Castle Street, Bray, Co. Wicklow.
Tel: (01) 2869215
Web: www.vikingtackle.ie

Dogs, Rods and Guns
South Quay, Wicklow Town,
Tel: (0404) 25558
Web: www.dogsrodsguns.com

Online Tackle Shops

www.mactackle.com

www.baumanns.ie

www.crabrock.com

www.vikingtackle.ie

www.henrystackleshop.com

www.dogsrodsguns.com

www.procast-angling.com

www.anglersworld.ie

www.homefieldandstream.com

www.irishflyfishingshop.com

www.trevsflyshop.com

www.leansmountworms.com

Fishing Diary

Anglers have kept fishing diaries for years, and all will agree that it has helped them to become more successful. Most guides and top anglers keep diaries to help them understand the areas they are fishing and predict the best times and days for fishing that particular area. By doing the same, we can all become more successful anglers.

The idea of a fishing diary is the same as any other diary; to help you record certain events and/or organise your time. It will provide you with a tool to make your own calculations on best fishing times, tides, seasons etc., for specific areas. For instance, I know many anglers that travel great distances to certain areas in Ireland at the exact same tidal day each year, as they have found it to be successful at this time each year. This is no coincidence, fish base their activities on the lunar calendar, and weather, environment and atmospheric conditions permitting, the fish can be found in the same place year after year.

A diary can also help you understand the activities of fish and conditions of fish stocks more clearly. When kept, the diary will show specific patterns in successful fishing trips and you can then start to look at the specifics and predict when the fishing will be good again and if the stocks are increasing or decreasing in your particular area.

A successful fishing trip hinges on numerous factors. Suitable and reliable tackle, transport and bait are some of the things that you will have control of, and these are as important as any other. However, you will not have control of the weather, atmospheric pressure, local environment, tides, sun rise/set, moon rise/set and the current stocks of fish. Therefore, if you have kept a good record of fishing expeditions in the past, you should be able to decide where to fish on any given day in order to have the most success.

Sunday	Location
28	Tide
Wind	Bait
Fish	Remarks

Monday	Location
29	Tide
Wind	Bait
Fish	Remarks

Tuesday	Location
30	Tide
Wind	Bait
Fish	Remarks

Wednesday	Location
31	Tide
Wind	Balt
Fish	Remarks

Thursday	Location
1	Tide
Wind	Bait
Fish	Remarks

Friday	Location
2	Tide
Wind	Bait
Fish	Remarks

Saturday	Location
3	Tide
Wind	Bait
Fish	Remarks

January 2009

Sunday	Location
4	Tide
Wind	Bait
Fish	Remarks

Monday	Location
5	Tide
Wind	Bait
Fish	Remarks

Tuesday	Location
6	Tide
Wind	Bait
Fish	Remarks

Wednesday	Location
7	Tide
Wind	Bait
Fish	Remarks

Thursday	Location
8	Tide
Wind	Bait
Fish	Remarks

Friday	Location
9	Tide
Wind	Bait
Fish	Remarks

Saturday	Location
10	Tide
Wind	Bait
Fish	Remarks

Sunday   Location

11   Tide

Wind   Bait

Fish   Remarks

Monday   Location

12   Tide

Wind   Bait

Fish   Remarks

Tuesday   Location

13   Tide

Wind   Bait

Fish   Remarks

Wednesday   Location

14   Tide

Wind   Bait

Fish   Remarks

Thursday   Location

15   Tide

Wind   Bait

Fish   Remarks

Friday   Location

16   Tide

Wind   Bait

Fish   Remarks

Saturday   Location

17   Tide

Wind   Bait

Fish   Remarks

January 2009

Sunday	Location
18	Tide
Wind	Bait
Fish	Remarks

Monday	Location
19	Tide
Wind	Bait
Fish	Remarks

Tuesday	Location
20	Tide
Wind	Bait
Fish	Remarks

Wednesday	Location
21	Tide
Wind	Bait
Fish	Remarks

Thursday	Location
22	Tide
Wind	Bait
Fish	Remarks

Friday	Location
23	Tide
Wind	Bait
Fish	Remarks

Saturday	Location
24	Tide
Wind	Bait
Fish	Remarks

Sunday	Location
25	Tide
Wind	Bait
Fish	Remarks

Monday	Location
26	Tide
Wind	Bait
Fish	Remarks

Tuesday	Location
27	Tide
Wind	Bait
Fish	Remarks

Wednesday	Location
28	Tide
Wind	Bait
Fish	Remarks

Thursday	Location
29	Tide
Wind	Bait
Fish	Remarks

Friday	Location
30	Tide
Wind	Bait
Fish	Remarks

Saturday	Location
31	Tide
Wind	Bait
Fish	Remarks

February 2009

Sunday	Location
1	Tide
Wind	Bait
Fish	Remarks

Monday	Location
2	Tide
Wind	Bait
Fish	Remarks

Tuesday	Location
3	Tide
Wind	Bait
Fish	Remarks

Wednesday	Location
4	Tide
Wind	Bait
Fish	Remarks

Thursday	Location
5	Tide
Wind	Bait
Fish	Remarks

Friday	Location
6	Tide
Wind	Bait
Fish	Remarks

Saturday	Location
7	Tide
Wind	Bait
Fish	Remarks

Sunday	Location
8	Tide
Wind	Bait
Fish	Remarks

Monday	Location
9	Tide
Wind	Bait
Fish	Remarks

Tuesday	Location
10	Tide
Wind	Bait
Fish	Remarks

Wednesday	Location
11	Tide
Wind	Bait
Fish	Remarks

Thursday	Location
12	Tide
Wind	Bait
Fish	Remarks

Friday	Location
13	Tide
Wind	Bait
Fish	Remarks

Saturday	Location
14	Tide
Wind	Bait
Fish	Remarks

February 2009

Sunday	Location
15	Tide
Wind	Bait
Fish	Remarks

Monday	Location
16	Tide
Wind	Bait
Fish	Remarks

Tuesday	Location
17	Tide
Wind	Bait
Fish	Remarks

Wednesday	Location
18	Tide
Wind	Bait
Fish	Remarks

Thursday	Location
19	Tide
Wind	Bait
Fish	Remarks

Friday	Location
20	Tide
Wind	Bait
Fish	Remarks

Saturday	Location
21	Tide
Wind	Bait
Fish	Remarks

Sunday	Location
22	Tide
Wind	Bait
Fish	Remarks

Monday	Location
23	Tide
Wind	Bait
Fish	Remarks

Tuesday	Location
24	Tide
Wind	Bait
Fish	Remarks

Wednesday	Location
25	Tide
Wind	Bait
Fish	Remarks

Thursday	Location
26	Tide
Wind	Bait
Fish	Remarks

Friday	Location
27	Tide
Wind	Bait
Fish	Remarks

Saturday	Location
28	Tide
Wind	Bait
Fish	Remarks

March 2009

Sunday	Location
1	Tide
Wind	Bait
Fish	Remarks

Monday	Location
2	Tide
Wind	Bait
Fish	Remarks

Tuesday	Location
3	Tide
Wind	Bait
Fish	Remarks

Wednesday	Location
4	Tide
Wind	Bait
Fish	Remarks

Thursday	Location
5	Tide
Wind	Bait
Fish	Remarks

Friday	Location
6	Tide
Wind	Bait
Fish	Remarks

Saturday	Location
7	Tide
Wind	Bait
Fish	Remarks

Sunday	Location
8	Tide
Wind	Bait
Fish	Remarks

Monday	Location
9	Tide
Wind	Bait
Fish	Remarks

Tuesday	Location
10	Tide
Wind	Bait
Fish	Remarks

Wednesday	Location
11	Tide
Wind	Bait
Fish	Remarks

Thursday	Location
12	Tide
Wind	Bait
Fish	Remarks

Friday	Location
13	Tide
Wind	Bait
Fish	Remarks

Saturday	Location
14	Tide
Wind	Bait
Fish	Remarks

March 2009

Sunday	Location
15	Tide
Wind	Bait
Fish	Remarks

Monday	Location
16	Tide
Wind	Bait
Fish	Remarks

Tuesday	Location
17	Tide
Wind	Bait
Fish	Remarks

Wednesday	Location
18	Tide
Wind	Bait
Fish	Remarks

Thursday	Location
19	Tide
Wind	Bait
Fish	Remarks

Friday	Location
20	Tide
Wind	Bait
Fish	Remarks

Saturday	Location
21	Tide
Wind	Bait
Fish	Remarks

Sunday	Location
22	Tide
Wind	Bait
Fish	Remarks

Monday	Location
23	Tide
Wind	Bait
Fish	Remarks

Tuesday	Location
24	Tide
Wind	Bait
Fish	Remarks

Wednesday	Location
25	Tide
Wind	Bait
Fish	Remarks

Thursday	Location
26	Tide
Wind	Bait
Fish	Remarks

Friday	Location
27	Tide
Wind	Bait
Fish	Remarks

Saturday	Location
28	Tide
Wind	Bait
Fish	Remarks

March/April 2009

Sunday	Location
29	Tide
Wind	Bait
Fish	Remarks

Monday	Location
30	Tide
Wind	Bait
Fish	Remarks

Tuesday	Location
31	Tide
Wind	Bait
Fish	Remarks

Wednesday	Location
1	Tide
Wind	Bait
Fish	Remarks

Thursday	Location
2	Tide
Wind	Bait
Fish	Remarks

Friday	Location
3	Tide
Wind	Bait
Fish	Remarks

Saturday	Location
4	Tide
Wind	Bait
Fish	Remarks

Sunday	Location
5	Tide
Wind	Bait
Fish	Remarks

Monday	Location
6	Tide
Wind	Bait
Fish	Remarks

Tuesday	Location
7	Tide
Wind	Bait
Fish	Remarks

Wednesday	Location
8	Tide
Wind	Bait
Fish	Remarks

Thursday	Location
9	Tide
Wind	Bait
Fish	Remarks

Friday	Location
10	Tide
Wind	Bait
Fish	Remarks

Saturday	Location
11	Tide
Wind	Bait
Fish	Remarks

April 2009

Sunday	Location	
12	Tide	
Wind	Bait	
Fish	Remarks	
Monday	Location	
13	Tide	
Wind	Bait	
Fish	Remarks	
Tuesday	Location	
14	Tide	
Wind	Bait	
Fish	Remarks	
Wednesday	Location	
15	Tide	
Wind	Bait	
Fish	Remarks	
Thursday	Location	
16	Tide	
Wind	Bait	
Fish	Remarks	
Friday	Location	
17	Tide	
Wind	Bait	
Fish	Remarks	
Saturday	Location	
18	Tide	
Wind	Bait	
Fish	Remarks	

Sunday	Location
19	Tide
Wind	Bait
Fish	Remarks

Monday	Location
20	Tide
Wind	Bait
Fish	Remarks

Tuesday	Location
21	Tide
Wind	Bait
Fish	Remarks

Wednesday	Location
22	Tide
Wind	Bait
Fish	Remarks

Thursday	Location
23	Tide
Wind	Bait
Fish	Remarks

Friday	Location
24	Tide
Wind	Bait
Fish	Remarks

Saturday	Location
25	Tide
Wind	Bait
Fish	Remarks

April/May 2009

Sunday	Location
26	Tide
Wind	Bait
Fish	Remarks

Monday	Location
27	Tide
Wind	Bait
Fish	Remarks

Tuesday	Location
28	Tide
Wind	Bait
Fish	Remarks

Wednesday	Location
29	Tide
Wind	Bait
Fish	Remarks

Thursday	Location
30	Tide
Wind	Bait
Fish	Remarks

Friday	Location
1	Tide
Wind	Bait
Fish	Remarks

Saturday	Location
2	Tide
Wind	Bait
Fish	Remarks

Sunday	Location
3	Tide
Wind	Bait
Fish	Remarks
Monday	Location
4	Tide
Wind	Bait
Fish	Remarks
Tuesday	Location
5	Tide
Wind	Bait
Fish	Remarks
Wednesday	Location
6	Tide
Wind	Bait
Fish	Remarks
Thursday	Location
7	Tide
Wind	Bait
Fish	Remarks
Friday	Location
8	Tide
Wind	Bait
Fish	Remarks
Saturday	Location
9	Tide
Wind	Bait
Fish	Remarks

May 2009

Sunday	Location
10	Tide
Wind	Bait
Fish	Remarks

Monday	Location
11	Tide
Wind	Bait
Fish	Remarks

Tuesday	Location
12	Tide
Wind	Bait
Fish	Remarks

Wednesday	Location
13	Tide
Wind	Bait
Fish	Remarks

Thursday	Location
14	Tide
Wind	Bait
Fish	Remarks

Friday	Location
15	Tide
Wind	Bait
Fish	Remarks

Saturday	Location
16	Tide
Wind	Bait
Fish	Remarks

Sunday	Location
17	Tide
Wind	Bait
Fish	Remarks

Monday	Location
18	Tide
Wind	Bait
Fish	Remarks

Tuesday	Location
19	Tide
Wind	Bait
Fish	Remarks

Wednesday	Location
20	Tide
Wind	Bait
Fish	Remarks

Thursday	Location
21	Tide
Wind	Bait
Fish	Remarks

Friday	Location
22	Tide
Wind	Bait
Fish	Remarks

Saturday	Location
23	Tide
Wind	Bait
Fish	Remarks

May 2009

Sunday	Location
24	Tide
Wind	Bait
Fish	Remarks

Monday	Location
25	Tide
Wind	Bait
Fish	Remarks

Tuesday	Location
26	Tide
Wind	Bait
Fish	Remarks

Wednesday	Location
27	Tide
Wind	Bait
Fish	Remarks

Thursday	Location
28	Tide
Wind	Bait
Fish	Remarks

Friday	Location
29	Tide
Wind	Bait
Fish	Remarks

Saturday	Location
30	Tide
Wind	Bait
Fish	Remarks

Sunday	Location
31	Tide
Wind	Bait
Fish	Remarks
Monday	Location
1	Tide
Wind	Bait
Fish	Remarks
Tuesday	Location
2	Tide
Wind	Bait
Fish	Remarks
Wednesday	Location
3	Tide
Wind	Bait
Fish	Remarks
Thursday	Location
4	Tide
Wind	Bait
Fish	Remarks
Friday	Location
5	Tide
Wind	Bait
Fish	Remarks
Saturday	Location
6	Tide
Wind	Bait
Fish	Remarks

June 2009

Sunday	Location
7	Tide
Wind	Bait
Fish	Remarks

Monday	Location
8	Tide
Wind	Bait
Fish	Remarks

Tuesday	Location
9	Tide
Wind	Bait
Fish	Remarks

Wednesday	Location
10	Tide
Wind	Bait
Fish	Remarks

Thursday	Location
11	Tide
Wind	Bait
Fish	Remarks

Friday	Location
12	Tide
Wind	Bait
Fish	Remarks

Saturday	Location
13	Tide
Wind	Bait
Fish	Remarks

Sunday	Location
14	Tide
Wind	Bait
Fish	Remarks

Monday	Location
15	Tide
Wind	Bait
Fish	Remarks

Tuesday	Location
16	Tide
Wind	Bait
Fish	Remarks

Wednesday	Location
17	Tide
Wind	Bait
Fish	Remarks

Thursday	Location
18	Tide
Wind	Bait
Fish	Remarks

Friday	Location
19	Tide
Wind	Bait
Fish	Remarks

Saturday	Location
20	Tide
Wind	Bait
Fish	Remarks

June 2009

Sunday	Location
21	Tide
Wind	Bait
Fish	Remarks
Monday	Location
22	Tide
Wind	Bait
Fish	Remarks
Tuesday	Location
23	Tide
Wind	Bait
Fish	Remarks
Wednesday	Location
24	Tide
Wind	Bait
Fish	Remarks
Thursday	Location
25	Tide
Wind	Bait
Fish	Remarks
Friday	Location
26	Tide
Wind	Bait
Fish	Remarks
Saturday	Location
27	Tide
Wind	Bait
Fish	Remarks

Sunday
Location

28
Tide

Wind
Bait

Fish
Remarks

Monday
Location

29
Tide

Wind
Bait

Fish
Remarks

Tuesday
Location

30
Tide

Wind
Bait

Fish
Remarks

Wednesday
Location

1
Tide

Wind
Bait

Fish
Remarks

Thursday
Location

2
Tide

Wind
Bait

Fish
Remarks

Friday
Location

3
Tide

Wind
Bait

Fish
Remarks

Saturday
Location

4
Tide

Wind
Bait

Fish
Remarks

July 2009

Sunday	Location
5	Tide
Wind	Bait
Fish	Remarks

Monday	Location
6	Tide
Wind	Bait
Fish	Remarks

Tuesday	Location
7	Tide
Wind	Bait
Fish	Remarks

Wednesday	Location
8	Tide
Wind	Bait
Fish	Remarks

Thursday	Location
9	Tide
Wind	Bait
Fish	Remarks

Friday	Location
10	Tide
Wind	Bait
Fish	Remarks

Saturday	Location
11	Tide
Wind	Bait
Fish	Remarks

Sunday	Location
12	Tide
Wind	Bait
Fish	Remarks

Monday	Location
13	Tide
Wind	Bait
Fish	Remarks

Tuesday	Location
14	Tide
Wind	Bait
Fish	Remarks

Wednesday	Location
15	Tide
Wind	Bait
Fish	Remarks

Thursday	Location
16	Tide
Wind	Bait
Fish	Remarks

Friday	Location
17	Tide
Wind	Bait
Fish	Remarks

Saturday	Location
18	Tide
Wind	Bait
Fish	Remarks

July 2009

Sunday	Location
19	Tide
Wind	Bait
Fish	Remarks

Monday	Location
20	Tide
Wind	Bait
Fish	Remarks

Tuesday	Location
21	Tide
Wind	Bait
Fish	Remarks

Wednesday	Location
22	Tide
Wind	Bait
Fish	Remarks

Thursday	Location
23	Tide
Wind	Bait
Fish	Remarks

Friday	Location
24	Tide
Wind	Bait
Fish	Remarks

Saturday	Location
25	Tide
Wind	Bait
Fish	Remarks

Sunday	Location
26	Tide
Wind	Bait
Fish	Remarks

Monday	Location
27	Tide
Wind	Bait
Fish	Remarks

Tuesday	Location
28	Tide
Wind	Bait
Fish	Remarks

Wednesday	Location
29	Tide
Wind	Bait
Fish	Remarks

Thursday	Location
30	Tide
Wind	Bait
Fish	Remarks

Friday	Location
31	Tide
Wind	Bait
Fish	Remarks

Saturday	Location
1	Tide
Wind	Bait
Fish	Remarks

August 2009

Sunday	Location
2	Tide
Wind	Bait
Fish	Remarks

Monday	Location
3	Tide
Wind	Bait
Fish	Remarks

Tuesday	Location
4	Tide
Wind	Bait
Fish	Remarks

Wednesday	Location
5	Tide
Wind	Bait
Fish	Remarks

Thursday	Location
6	Tide
Wind	Bait
Fish	Remarks

Friday	Location
7	Tide
Wind	Bait
Fish	Remarks

Saturday	Location
8	Tide
Wind	Bait
Fish	Remarks

Sunday	Location
9	Tide
Wind	Bait
Fish	Remarks

Monday	Location
10	Tide
Wind	Bait
Fish	Remarks

Tuesday	Location
11	Tide
Wind	Bait
Fish	Remarks

Wednesday	Location
12	Tide
Wind	Bait
Fish	Remarks

Thursday	Location
13	Tide
Wind	Bait
Fish	Remarks

Friday	Location
14	Tide
Wind	Bait
Fish	Remarks

Saturday	Location
15	Tide
Wind	Bait
Fish	Remarks

August 2009

Sunday	Location
16	Tide
Wind	Bait
Fish	Remarks

Monday	Location
17	Tide
Wind	Bait
Fish	Remarks

Tuesday	Location
18	Tide
Wind	Bait
Fish	Remarks

Wednesday	Location
19	Tide
Wind	Bait
Fish	Remarks

Thursday	Location
20	Tide
Wind	Bait
Fish	Remarks

Friday	Location
21	Tide
Wind	Bait
Fish	Remarks

Saturday	Location
22	Tide
Wind	Bait
Fish	Remarks

Sunday	Location
23	Tide
Wind	Bait
Fish	Remarks

Monday	Location
24	Tide
Wind	Bait
Fish	Remarks

Tuesday	Location
25	Tide
Wind	Bait
Fish	Remarks

Wednesday	Location
26	Tide
Wind	Balt
Fish	Remarks

Thursday	Location
27	Tide
Wind	Bait
Fish	Remarks

Friday	Location
28	Tide
Wind	Bait
Fish	Remarks

Saturday	Location
29	Tide
Wind	Bait
Fish	Remarks

Sunday	Location
30	Tide
Wind	Bait
Fish	Remarks
Monday	Location
31	Tide
Wind	Bait
Fish	Remarks
Tuesday	Location
1	Tide
Wind	Bait
Fish	Remarks
Wednesday	Location
2	Tide
Wind	Bait
Fish	Remarks
Thursday	Location
3	Tide
Wind	Bait
Fish	Remarks
Friday	Location
4	Tide
Wind	Bait
Fish	Remarks
Saturday	Location
5	Tide
Wind	Bait
Fish	Remarks

Sunday	Location
6	Tide
Wind	Bait
Fish	Remarks

Monday	Location
7	Tide
Wind	Bait
Fish	Remarks

Tuesday	Location
8	Tide
Wind	Bait
Fish	Remarks

Wednesday	Location
9	Tide
Wind	Balt
Fish	Remarks

Thursday	Location
10	Tide
Wind	Bait
Fish	Remarks

Friday	Location
11	Tide
Wind	Bait
Fish	Remarks

Saturday	Location
12	Tide
Wind	Bait
Fish	Remarks

September 2009

Sunday	Location
13	Tide
Wind	Bait
Fish	Remarks

Monday	Location
14	Tide
Wind	Bait
Fish	Remarks

Tuesday	Location
15	Tide
Wind	Bait
Fish	Remarks

Wednesday	Location
16	Tide
Wind	Bait
Fish	Remarks

Thursday	Location
17	Tide
Wind	Bait
Fish	Remarks

Friday	Location
18	Tide
Wind	Bait
Fish	Remarks

Saturday	Location
19	Tide
Wind	Bait
Fish	Remarks

Sunday	Location
20	Tide
Wind	Bait
Fish	Remarks

Monday	Location
21	Tide
Wind	Bait
Fish	Remarks

Tuesday	Location
22	Tide
Wind	Bait
Fish	Remarks

Wednesday	Location
23	Tide
Wind	Bait
Fish	Remarks

Thursday	Location
24	Tide
Wind	Bait
Fish	Remarks

Friday	Location
25	Tide
Wind	Bait
Fish	Remarks

Saturday	Location
26	Tide
Wind	Bait
Fish	Remarks

September/October 2009

Sunday	Location
27	Tide
Wind	Bait
Fish	Remarks

Monday	Location
28	Tide
Wind	Bait
Fish	Remarks

Tuesday	Location
29	Tide
Wind	Bait
Fish	Remarks

Wednesday	Location
30	Tide
Wind	Bait
Fish	Remarks

Thursday	Location
1	Tide
Wind	Bait
Fish	Remarks

Friday	Location
2	Tide
Wind	Bait
Fish	Remarks

Saturday	Location
3	Tide
Wind	Bait
Fish	Remarks

Sunday	Location
4	Tide
Wind	Bait
Fish	Remarks

Monday	Location
5	Tide
Wind	Bait
Fish	Remarks

Tuesday	Location
6	Tide
Wind	Bait
Fish	Remarks

Wednesday	Location
7	Tide
Wind	Bait
Fish	Remarks

Thursday	Location
8	Tide
Wind	Bait
Fish	Remarks

Friday	Location
9	Tide
Wind	Bait
Fish	Remarks

Saturday	Location
10	Tide
Wind	Bait
Fish	Remarks

October 2009

Sunday	Location
11	Tide
Wind	Bait
Fish	Remarks

Monday	Location
12	Tide
Wind	Bait
Fish	Remarks

Tuesday	Location
13	Tide
Wind	Bait
Fish	Remarks

Wednesday	Location
14	Tide
Wind	Bait
Fish	Remarks

Thursday	Location
15	Tide
Wind	Bait
Fish	Remarks

Friday	Location
16	Tide
Wind	Bait
Fish	Remarks

Saturday	Location
17	Tide
Wind	Bait
Fish	Remarks

Sunday	Location
18	Tide
Wind	Bait
Fish	Remarks

Monday	Location
19	Tide
Wind	Bait
Fish	Remarks

Tuesday	Location
20	Tide
Wind	Bait
Fish	Remarks

Wednesday	Location
21	Tide
Wind	Bait
Fish	Remarks

Thursday	Location
22	Tide
Wind	Bait
Fish	Remarks

Friday	Location
23	Tide
Wind	Bait
Fish	Remarks

Saturday	Location
24	Tide
Wind	Bait
Fish	Remarks

October 2009

Sunday	Location
25	Tide
Wind	Bait
Fish	Remarks

Monday	Location
26	Tide
Wind	Bait
Fish	Remarks

Tuesday	Location
27	Tide
Wind	Bait
Fish	Remarks

Wednesday	Location
28	Tide
Wind	Bait
Fish	Remarks

Thursday	Location
29	Tide
Wind	Bait
Fish	Remarks

Friday	Location
30	Tide
Wind	Bait
Fish	Remarks

Saturday	Location
31	Tide
Wind	Bait
Fish	Remarks

Sunday	Location
1	Tide
Wind	Bait
Fish	Remarks
Monday	Location
2	Tide
Wind	Bait
Fish	Remarks
Tuesday	Location
3	Tide
Wind	Bait
Fish	Remarks
Wednesday	Location
4	Tide
Wind	Bait
Fish	Remarks
Thursday	Location
5	Tide
Wind	Bait
Fish	Remarks
Friday	Location
6	Tide
Wind	Bait
Fish	Remarks
Saturday	Location
7	Tide
Wind	Bait
Fish	Remarks

November 2009

Sunday	Location
8	Tide
Wind	Bait
Fish	Remarks

Monday	Location
9	Tide
Wind	Bait
Fish	Remarks

Tuesday	Location
10	Tide
Wind	Bait
Fish	Remarks

Wednesday	Location
11	Tide
Wind	Bait
Fish	Remarks

Thursday	Location
12	Tide
Wind	Bait
Fish	Remarks

Friday	Location
13	Tide
Wind	Bait
Fish	Remarks

Saturday	Location
14	Tide
Wind	Bait
Fish	Remarks

Sunday

15

Wind

Fish

Location

Tide

Bait

Remarks

Monday

16

Wind

Fish

Location

Tide

Bait

Remarks

Tuesday

17

Wind

Fish

Location

Tide

Bait

Remarks

Wednesday

18

Wind

Fish

Location

Tide

Bait

Remarks

Thursday

19

Wind

Fish

Location

Tide

Bait

Remarks

Friday

20

Wind

Fish

Location

Tide

Bait

Remarks

Saturday

21

Wind

Fish

Location

Tide

Bait

Remarks

November 2009

Sunday	Location
22	Tide
Wind	Bait
Fish	Remarks

Monday	Location
23	Tide
Wind	Bait
Fish	Remarks

Tuesday	Location
24	Tide
Wind	Bait
Fish	Remarks

Wednesday	Location
25	Tide
Wind	Bait
Fish	Remarks

Thursday	Location
26	Tide
Wind	Bait
Fish	Remarks

Friday	Location
27	Tide
Wind	Bait
Fish	Remarks

Saturday	Location
28	Tide
Wind	Bait
Fish	Remarks

Sunday	Location
29	Tide
Wind	Bait
Fish	Remarks

Monday	Location
30	Tide
Wind	Bait
Fish	Remarks

Tuesday	Location
1	Tide
Wind	Bait
Fish	Remarks

Wednesday	Location
2	Tide
Wind	Bait
Fish	Remarks

Thursday	Location
3	Tide
Wind	Bait
Fish	Remarks

Friday	Location
4	Tide
Wind	Bait
Fish	Remarks

Saturday	Location
5	Tide
Wind	Bait
Fish	Remarks

December 2009

Sunday	Location
6	Tide
Wind	Bait
Fish	Remarks

Monday	Location
7	Tide
Wind	Bait
Fish	Remarks

Tuesday	Location
8	Tide
Wind	Bait
Fish	Remarks

Wednesday	Location
9	Tide
Wind	Bait
Fish	Remarks

Thursday	Location
10	Tide
Wind	Bait
Fish	Remarks

Friday	Location
11	Tide
Wind	Bait
Fish	Remarks

Saturday	Location
12	Tide
Wind	Bait
Fish	Remarks

Sunday	Location
13	Tide
Wind	Bait
Fish	Remarks

Monday	Location
14	Tide
Wind	Bait
Fish	Remarks

Tuesday	Location
15	Tide
Wind	Bait
Fish	Remarks

Wednesday	Location
16	Tide
Wind	Bait
Fish	Remarks

Thursday	Location
17	Tide
Wind	Bait
Fish	Remarks

Friday	Location
18	Tide
Wind	Bait
Fish	Remarks

Saturday	Location
19	Tide
Wind	Bait
Fish	Remarks

December 2009

Sunday	Location	
20	Tide	
Wind	Bait	
Fish	Remarks	

Monday	Location	
21	Tide	
Wind	Bait	
Fish	Remarks	

Tuesday	Location	
22	Tide	
Wind	Bait	
Fish	Remarks	

Wednesday	Location	
23	Tide	
Wind	Bait	
Fish	Remarks	

Thursday	Location	
24	Tide	
Wind	Bait	
Fish	Remarks	

Friday	Location	
25	Tide	
Wind	Bait	
Fish	Remarks	

Saturday	Location	
26	Tide	
Wind	Bait	
Fish	Remarks	

Sunday	Location
27	Tide
Wind	Bait
Fish	Remarks

Monday	Location
28	Tide
Wind	Bait
Fish	Remarks

Tuesday	Location
29	Tide
Wind	Bait
Fish	Remarks

Wednesday	Location
30	Tide
Wind	Bait
Fish	Remarks

Thursday	Location
31	Tide
Wind	Bait
Fish	Remarks

Friday	Location
1	Tide
Wind	Bait
Fish	Remarks

Saturday	Location
2	Tide
Wind	Bait
Fish	Remarks

Tight Lines